Restorative Justice Conferencing
◆◆◆

Real Justice® & The Conferencing Handbook

by
Ted Wachtel
Terry O'Connell
Ben Wachtel

INTERNATIONAL INSTITUTE FOR RESTORATIVE PRACTICES
Bethlehem, Pennsylvania, USA

published in collaboration with

THE PIPER'S PRESS
Pipersville, Pennsylvania, USA

RESTORATIVE JUSTICE CONFERENCING:
REAL JUSTICE® & THE CONFERENCING HANDBOOK
Copyright © 2010 The Piper's Press
All Rights Reserved

10 9 8 7 6 5 4 3 2 1
FIRST EDITION
Printed in Canada

INTERNATIONAL INSTITUTE FOR RESTORATIVE PRACTICES
P.O. Box 229
Bethlehem, PA 18016 USA

Published in collaboration with
THE PIPER'S PRESS
P.O. Box 400
Pipersville, PA 18947 USA

BOOK AND COVER DESIGN
Christopher MacDonald

Library of Congress Control Number: 2010926941
ISBN-13: 978-1-934355-03-9
ISBN-10: 1-934355-03-8

In memory of Ali Thurman Bonner
who served his time by turning
his life to the service of others

Table of Contents

REAL JUSTICE   How We Can Revolutionize Our Response to Wrongdoing

Preface

This book combines two books previously published separately by The Piper's Press into one volume. The first book, *Real Justice* (originally published in 1997), by Ted Wachtel, demonstrates how restorative justice conferencing benefits victims, offenders and the community by actively involving those affected by wrongdoing in the process of repairing the harm and by fostering the closure and the emotional healing that is largely denied in our current systems. Wachtel, who founded the Real Justice movement in 1995, uses actual conference stories to show how conferencing works and how it can change the way our society responds to wrongdoing in schools, criminal justice, the workplace and elsewhere.

The second book, *Conferencing Handbook* (originally published in 1999 as *Conferencing Handbook: The New Real Justice Training Manual*), by Ted Wachtel, Terry O'Connell and Ben Wachtel, is a step-by-step guide to facilitating conferences in school, criminal justice and other settings. The handbook covers the process of selecting cases, inviting participants, making preparations and running the conference itself. Co-author Terry O'Connell developed the restorative conference "script" while serving as a police sergeant in New South Wales, Australia. (A printable version of the script can be downloaded at: www.realjustice.org/pdf/script.pdf.)

Real Justice®

How We Can Revolutionize Our Response to Wrongdoing

by
Ted Wachtel

CHAPTER 1

Uncle Marty's Sneaker Barn Burglary

Summer, 1978

Marty Stern, looking angry and frustrated as the juvenile court hearing proceeded, sat on the opposite side of the courtroom from me. His wife, Sharon, seemed to share his feelings but she was pre-occupied with their baby daughter. I had first noticed them when they arrived that morning. I watched them throughout the day as they waited uncomfortably in the crowded hallway outside the courtroom. Marty looked at his watch again and again. Apparently no one had told him that the "nine o'clock" time cited in the hearing notification letter was the time when the juvenile court judge started hearing cases, not when the court would deal with his case. The hearing for the burglary of his retail store, "Uncle Marty's Sneaker Barn," would not occur until late afternoon.

I was as poorly informed as Marty. This was my first juvenile court hearing. As a former public school teacher I had no experience with juvenile court procedures. I was attending as a representative of the Community Service Foundation, the small school and counseling agency for troubled youth that my wife and I had established just a few months before the hearing. Two of our students, a teenage boy and girl, along with several other teen-agers, were charged with burglarizing Marty's store.

Marty Stern also had been a public school teacher at a local high school, as well as a track coach, before opening his own retail store. As most citizens would, he expected the court to provide him with an opportunity for justice. The young burglars had waited all day in the same hallway, not far from Marty and his family. It seemed strange to me that the teen-agers were not accompanied by their parents. In the morning they seemed scared, talking nervously and smoking lots of cigarettes. Ironically, the wait outside the courtroom brought them together to plan their defense, something they never would have accomplished through their own initiative. Now they had more than six hours to contrive excuses and attempt to minimize their involvement. As the day wore on they seemed to get increasingly cocky, convincing themselves that they were going to talk their way out of their troubles.

Then, at three o'clock in the afternoon, the hearing was convened in the small courtroom used for juvenile cases. Although they were the victims, Marty and Sharon Stern had no role in the process. A police officer provided the factual information so Marty and Sharon, the proprietors of Uncle Marty's Sneaker Barn, had no occasion to speak.

The public defender did most of the talking for the offenders. When the youths did speak, their obvious attempts to minimize or abdicate responsibility were ignored by the judge, because he did not believe them. The judge put all the offenders on probation, extending the probation period for one boy who was already on probation, and remanded our two students back to our school, where they had been attending voluntarily since first being charged with the offense.

After spending a day in the courthouse hallway anticipating what they hoped would be a meaningful process, Marty and Sharon experienced a court proceeding in which they had no role and which ended with ambiguous results and unanswered questions. They wondered: "What does it mean to be on juvenile probation? What does it mean for two offenders to be sent back to a school for troubled students that they were already attending? What about restitution? What about Marty's trophies and medals that were stolen? What about our feelings? Why did we spend the day waiting in the courthouse? Why weren't we asked to say anything? What just happened?"

After the Uncle Marty's Sneaker Barn burglary hearing, I left the courtroom feeling terrible. I couldn't stop thinking about how isolated and confused Marty and Sharon seemed. I could only imagine how badly they must have felt. Late that night I found myself tossing and turning in my bed, still so disturbed by my experience in court that I could not sleep.

Finally, in the middle of the night, I decided to write to them. I felt I was taking a risk, that perhaps my letter would be misunderstood or unappreciated. Or perhaps they would see me as just another person in the juvenile justice system who had failed to meet their expectations.

I wrote to them about my own disappointment and dismay at how the court process failed to meet my expectations of justice. I told them how badly I felt watching them endure a day of waiting and then a hearing that seemed so incomplete and unsatisfying. I offered my condolences so that they knew that someone else recognized their plight as crime victims in an insensitive justice system.

A couple of days later, Marty responded with a phone call, and we got together to talk. Although I had little but my empathy to offer, he seemed to appreciate that I noticed and acknowledged his feelings and his frustration. Marty explained that he went to court that day not seeking revenge or severe punishment for the youths.

What he had hoped to get in court was a chance to talk to the kids and let them know how he felt. He particularly wanted to ask them to return one gold medal they had stolen. That medal and other trophies of his college track career had been on display in his store to confirm his credibility as a track star and coach. All the stolen merchandise and all the trophies were of less consequence to him than that one gold medal, a memento of his first triumph in college track.

But the court neither provided him with an opportunity to talk directly to the youths nor with a feeling of justice.

After my meeting with Marty, whenever I shopped at Uncle Marty's Sneaker Barn with my family, he always greeted us warmly and insisted on giving us a generous discount on sneakers. He also gave us Uncle Marty's Sneaker Barn T-shirts as gifts, which for many years served to remind me of that awful day in court.

As for the two young burglars who attended our school, their experience in court produced nothing positive. They failed to demonstrate respect for the court or the victim. Both the boy and the girl avoided their feelings by making light of the experience. For some time after the court hearing I would hear them ridiculing the judge and "Uncle Marty."

One afternoon I gave the boy a ride home from school and made an impassioned appeal for the gold medal that he and his friends had stolen. I tried to get him to empathize with Marty's feelings and I sensed that he did feel badly. But he seemed afraid to say anything.

In the years to come I would become more experienced in addressing the inappropriate attitudes and behaviors I encountered in the two students. At that time I was only a novice counselor and handled the whole situation with them in a clumsy and unproductive manner.

Marty Stern later returned to a successful career coaching college track at Villanova University. I remember my delight at seeing him interviewed on television when he was coaching American athletes participating in the Olympics.

CHAPTER 2

Stealing the Crime ·

Summer, 1997

Many years have passed, and our Community Service Foundation has grown to five schools, eight group homes and other programs aimed at changing the negative behavior of young people who are in trouble. But I have never forgotten the Uncle Marty's Sneaker Barn burglary and that feeling of my heart sinking at the court hearing when I first realized that our criminal justice system does not provide real justice.

If the Uncle Marty's Sneaker Barn burglary hearing had been held today rather than in 1978, the court's victim-witness coordinator would have answered many of the Stern family's questions, a clear improvement over their experience that day. In some juvenile courts today they might be asked to submit a victim-impact statement, which would allow them some limited input into the decision-making process, but in other locales the judge might not ask for their input and might not even allow them into the courtroom. The criminal justice system neither serves the needs of crime victims nor provides them with a significant role in the process.

When victims do attend court, they may provide testimony but are not permitted to talk directly to offenders. They can only listen to what offenders say when asked direct questions by attorneys or the judge. But defense lawyers curtail what defendants say and do much of the talking for them. Victims are usually unable to resolve their own emotional concerns or get the answer to the question many of them long to ask the offenders: "Why me? Why did you do this to me?"

In effect, the court steals the crime from the victim. The process focuses on determining the guilt of the offender or meting out punishment. Although the victim suffered the crime, the court defines the offense as a crime against the state and gives the judge and jury the right to be lenient or strict, to dismiss consequences for the offender or order serious punishment. Victims neither determine nor have a significant say in the outcome.

Our criminal justice system places greater emphasis on the needs of the offenders than on those of the victims because many of its practices developed out of concern for protecting the accused individual from the abuse of power by the state. English law and our own American tradition contain numerous safeguards for the rights of defendants in criminal cases. Evidence can be ruled inadmissible if obtained improperly. Offenders cannot be forced to testify against themselves. There is no equivalent tradition of concern for the protection of victims, so they are largely neglected in the criminal court process.

Furthermore, courts deal with crimes as matters of fact and evidence, with little or no regard for the emotional consequences of the crime. That is why legal proceedings usually leave victims unsatisfied and unresolved. Their needs are primarily emotional, but they have no forum in which to resolve those needs and attain closure.

When the judge transferred the Oklahoma City federal building bombing trials to Denver in February 1996, he refused to allow closed-circuit television in Oklahoma so that victims and surviving family members could observe the trial. When Congress and the president made a law requiring a closed-circuit broadcast, the judge allowed only a 330-seat facility in Oklahoma City for the nearly 2,500 injured victims and surviving relatives. The victims each had to call a phone number to make a reservation for seating for one day at a time. The severely restricted seating was rotated among the large number of victims and survivors. Only a fraction of the group was able to observe the trial on any given day. The judge also assigned a retired judge to preside over the auditorium, hundreds of miles from the trial, to assure that spectators were quiet and that there was no crying.

At the 1995 O.J. Simpson murder trial the victim's sister, Kimberly Goldman, reported that had she left the trial to avoid crying during very emotional testimony she would have lost her seat. Had she brought tissues to the court they would have been confiscated as contraband.

While a crime impacts the primary victim most severely, the offense creates an emotional ripple that affects the victim's family and friends, the victim's neighbors and the community-at-large because the incident undermines feelings of safety and well-being. Courts disregard this widespread emotional impact and focus on the narrow concerns of evidence and due process. Through their lack of sensitivity to the needs of victims, their families and others impacted by the crime, courts frequently revictimize the victims and increase the psychological and emotional damage.

Victims cannot even count on seeing the offenders punished in the current system. Public prosecutors often dismiss cases because they feel they cannot win them or bargain with defense attorneys, settling for probation or a short prison sentence in exchange for a guilty plea. Victims are often the last to know the outcome.

A woman who was part of a panel of five parents and spouses of murder victims related how, in reading the morning paper, she learned that her husband's murderer had received a plea-bargained five-year sentence (of which he served only two years). She had been told earlier by the prosecuting attorney that he had a strong case. No one from the court even had the courtesy to give her a telephone call. Criminal justice professionals are not evil, but at times they are thoughtless. They have been trained and have worked in a system that was not designed to serve victims.

Nor are victims' physical losses or damages dealt with effectively. Even with the creation of state victim-compensation programs to reimburse victims, restitution can be haphazard, unreliable and unnecessarily marked by bureaucratic hassle.

Courts are all about determining guilt and handing out punishment. They are not about healing or repairing the harm. So something else, besides the court process, needs to happen to achieve real justice for victims, their families and the community.

CHAPTER 3

Cop from Wagga Wagga

Summer, 1994

By the time the cop from Wagga Wagga finished telling about the "Outback Vandals" and the "Roadhouse Thief," I knew that I would be going to Australia. I was encouraged by the hopefulness of his stories of restorative conferencing in contrast to my own experiences with the justice system, which included the Uncle Marty's Sneaker Barn burglary hearing.

Terry O'Connell, an Australian police sergeant, was speaking at a luncheon in Doylestown, Pennsylvania, sponsored by the Bucks County Juvenile Court and a local alternative school, in July 1994. He was visiting the United States, Canada, the United Kingdom and South Africa on a Winston Churchill Fellowship, which he had been awarded for his development of a new response to juvenile crime and school misconduct called the "family group conference" (also called a "community accountability conference" or "diversionary conference," and which we now call a "restorative conference").

The family group conference originated in New Zealand as part of the Children, Youth and Families Act of 1989. That legislation borrowed from the Maori, the indigenous people of New Zealand, the idea of bringing together the extended family of a young offender to decide how to deal with that young person's inappropriate behavior. The new law reflected the Maori tradition that the individual's family and community should be directly involved in any response to wrongdoing, a practice typical of most aboriginal or indigenous people's response to crime.

Terry O'Connell, living across the Tasman Sea in Australia, borrowed the concept and kept the name "family group conference," but changed the procedure substantially when he adapted it to community policing in Wagga Wagga, New South Wales. Having a police officer facilitate the conference, rather than a social worker, was distinctly different from the New Zealand approach. Terry also created a written script for the facilitator to follow, which he carefully revised as he gained experience with conferencing. The script made it much easier to conduct conferences and helped ensure a reliable result. The Wagga model of conferencing also gave the victim and victim's family and friends a much greater role than the New Zealand process.

What O'Connell devised in 1991 was a carefully orchestrated emotional encounter among young offenders, their victims and their respective friends and families that typically results in a written plan to repair the harm caused by the offense. When victims and other conference participants began singing the praises of conferencing, the practice spread. The Australian media started reporting about conferences. Australian educators began using the process with incidents of school misconduct in 1994. Young offenders, if they agreed to participate, were diverted from the normal court or school disciplinary procedures.

Below are two stories Terry O'Connell told at his presentation. I found myself listening, with tears in my eyes, as he described a better way of responding to young offenders and their crimes.

Outback Vandals

A police sergeant returned to his rural community in the Australian outback to a vandalism incident that had caused a local uproar. The four offenders were young blacks who lived in the town or at the nearby Aboriginal reserve (the equivalent of a U.S. Native American reservation or Canadian First Nations reserve). They had broken into the building occupied by an all-white women's organization and trashed the interior and its contents.

Having just attended training for a new response to wrongdoing called "conferencing," the officer saw the situation as a perfect opportunity to put his new skills into practice. He also hoped that the conference would address the heightened racial tension that was a by-product of the incident.

He first contacted the offenders and invited them, along with their families and friends, to meet with the vandalism victims "to find out what happened, see how people had been affected and decide how to repair the harm." He borrowed phrases he had just heard at the training to explain the process to the potential participants. When the offenders and their families accepted his offer of the conference, he then invited all of the women victims and their respective families and friends to participate.

The day of the conference was warm and sunny, typical of days in the Australian outback. This was fortunate because there were so many people in the offenders' and victims' groups that the conference had to be held outdoors. The chairs were arranged in a large circle, with the victims' group to the police officer's left and the offenders' group to the right.

The officer began by reminding all the participants that the conference was voluntary and that they could leave at any time. If the victims and offenders could reach an agreement, the matter could be settled then and there. The officer went around the group and introduced everyone. Then he asked each participant a series of questions.

First the offenders were asked to tell what happened. The youths were very forthcoming in admitting what they did and in expressing regret, which immediately reduced some of the bad feelings among the victims. When the boys were asked by the facilitating police officer, "What were you thinking about at the time?" they frankly admitted their resentment of the whites in their community, a prevalent feeling among blacks, but one which was rarely expressed aloud in the presence of the whites. When the officer asked "Who do you think has been affected?" they had only a very limited view of who and how others had been affected by their wrongdoing, as is usually the case with young offenders.

Then the women whose building had been vandalized related how the vandalism had affected them. They told the boys that they understood their resentment of whites, but they also admitted how uncomfortable and sometimes frightened they felt to be a small group of white people in a largely black community. Just like the black youths' resentment, the white women's feelings of fear and discomfort had rarely been expressed aloud in the presence of blacks.

Some of the victims also expressed anger, wondering if maybe the boys thought that white people could afford to repair the damage and that it would be no big deal. The most important issue, they explained, was not money; rather, the vandalism increased their fears and made them feel unsafe.

As the police officer worked his way around the group, husbands, children and friends expressed similar feelings of fear and anger. As the boys and their families listened respectfully, the intensity of the victims' group's feelings gradually subsided.

The boys' families responded very sympathetically to the victims. They apologized and expressed shame for what their children had done and promised it would not happen again. They also seemed genuinely surprised to hear about the fears and discomfort of the white minority in the community, having always felt that the whites had the upper hand. They understood how the vandalism had intensified those fears and wanted to help make things right.

By the time the conference turned to the issue of how to repair the harm, blacks and whites easily agreed to work together in the upcoming weekend to repair the damage to the building. Both groups had gained insight into each others' feelings. The young people now realized that they had not only damaged the property of a few people but also had affected a great many other people very deeply, including their own families.

The two groups, feeling separate from one another at the outset of the conference, now merged into one community. In the informal period after the conference, when refreshments were served, clusters of blacks and whites engaged in animated conversation. The vandalism incident had provided an opportunity for healing among people who had lived together for all of their lives without expressing their true feelings. In the safety of the conference, they had talked in a real way about how they felt toward one another and had taken significant steps toward mutual understanding.

Some of the influential blacks who lived on the reserve told the policeman how reluctant they were to call the police when there was a problem. They feared offenders would simply be locked away. They suggested that other crimes might be handled through a conference as a better response to problems on the reserve.

But I have saved the most ironic aspect of this story for last— the fact that the four vandals were only 5, 6, 7 and 8 years old. Under Australian law, the police officer had no real jurisdiction with children under 10 years old, since they were not considered responsible for their own actions. Having just learned how to facilitate a conference, however, he recognized that the process would allow him to deal with the bad feelings the incident had created in the community, even though he could not formally charge the offenders with a crime.

Had there been a number 1 in front of the boys' ages, had they been 15, 16, 17 and 18 years old, in the normal course of the criminal justice system all four would have been charged with crimes. All of them would have gone to juvenile court and none of them would have gained the kind of insight and empathy that they acquired through the conference. Blacks and whites in the community would have been left with their anger, fears and mutual resentments.

Roadhouse Thief

For months Walter, the owner of a roadhouse (an Australian term for a roadside convenience store) had noticed small amounts of money and items like cigarettes disappearing from his store. To some extent he had been in denial, finding it hard to believe that one of his employees might be a thief. Finally he secretly concealed a video camera in the store to catch the culprit on video.

Much to his surprise and chagrin he successfully videotaped Lou, a youth who worked for him, stealing a $20 bill from the drawer. Walter confronted Lou, who tearfully admitted to all of the thefts during the past months. Lou was the last person Walter would ever have imagined stealing from him. He was the son of a couple who were among his family's dearest friends. Nonetheless, Walter felt compelled to fire Lou from the job and call the police.

The arresting officer realized that calling the police had been a painful decision for Walter. The close relationship between Walter's and Lou's families and the youth's lack of a previous criminal record made the situation especially appropriate for a conference. Both parties agreed, and the policeman convened the conference a few days later in a room at the local police station.

Lou could not have been more ashamed. He knew that he had not only betrayed people who had always been kind and generous to him but also humiliated his own family and damaged the close relationship between Walter's family and his own.

The conference was an intensely emotional event. Walter and his wife repeatedly stated that they would never have expected Lou to be the thief and how betrayed and hurt they felt. They also pointed out the distance and discomfort between their two families since discovering who had been stealing from their store. Lou's parents echoed their friends' sentiments. They were utterly amazed that their son was capable of such wrongdoing and emphasized how ashamed and uncomfortable they felt talking to their longtime friends. They simply did not know what to say or how to make up for such a betrayal of friendship. Lou's siblings even felt ashamed at school and in town now that everyone knew their brother was a thief.

Expressing these feelings was helpful for both families and began the healing process between them. They next turned to discussing how to repair the harm and developed a written plan that satisfied all parties. As the conference reached its close, feelings eased and all acknowledged that while they disapproved of what Lou had done, they still cared about him and hoped that he would eventually restore trust within his own family and with the owner's family.

Because most crimes involve victims and offenders who live near each other and are likely to continue to see each other, punishing the offender is not enough. People need personal resolution so that they can deal with each other in the future. To prosecute the young roadhouse thief through the criminal justice system would have left two families who had long been friends in a very awkward situation, unable to resume their relationship. The conference provided a way to deal with those feelings, reconcile and move beyond the crisis while squarely addressing Lou's crime.

Epiphany

During Terry O'Connell's presentation I was seized by an "epiphany," a sudden intuitive realization that I had just encountered an essential universal truth. Conferencing was so simple that it was elegant, so basic that it was complete. Nothing in my experience with young offenders could match the positive outcomes being described by this Australian police officer. I wanted to bring conferencing to North America, where we lead the world in escalating juvenile crime and school misconduct. We have adopted the name "restorative conferencing" (after "restorative justice," which is discussed in Chapter 5) to differentiate the process from the original New Zealand family group conferencing model. We will use this term throughout the rest of this book.

The results with restorative conferencing were impressive. According to the Charles Sturt University study of the police experiment in Wagga Wagga, New South Wales, the number of juveniles who reoffended was half that of young offenders who were sent through the courts for the same offenses. More than 90 percent of the offenders who agreed to make cash restitution actually did so. Most significantly victims of crimes reported almost universal satisfaction with the outcomes of these restorative conferences.

O'Connell reassured the audience of judges, probation officers and police at the luncheon that the rights of both victims and offenders are scrupulously respected in his approach to conferencing. Accused youth must voluntarily agree to a conference, but only if they admit to the crime. A conference does not determine guilt or innocence. Offenders and victims may later change their decision and opt for a court trial, even during the conference itself, although that almost never happens.

The restorative conference provides a forum for everyone in the room to speak. Young offenders hear from those they have affected, unlike in the courtroom, where they routinely fail to recognize the implications and consequences of their behavior. I often asked young offenders who were returning to our school after a court hearing, "So how was court?"

"I dunno," they usually muttered. "It was OK."

Youth are largely unaffected by their court experience. The judge might give them a lecture, but they almost never hear from the people most affected by their behavior—the victims, the family and friends of victims, and their own family and friends. So they leave the courtroom without connecting anyone's feelings to their wrongdoing.

In the conference, however, they are directly confronted with other people's feelings. In the early stage of the conference they are asked, "Who do you think has been affected by your actions?" and their responses are remarkably limited. They don't seem to have a clue. But as the conference proceeds their awareness grows as they hear victims, victim supporters and then their own family members and friends share their feelings and their reactions. Each conference participant has an opportunity to speak.

Emotion gives the conference its power. The feelings of family members or friends have impact. For example, the offender's young sibling might say how much he loves the offender but hates what she has done. Tears surge to the eyes of everyone in the room, and the child's words touch the heart of the offender. Learning how their behavior affects others builds empathy in young offenders.

In the last phase of the conference, victims are asked what outcome they would like from the conference, and the offenders are asked to respond to what the victims have requested. Victims may want only an apology or ask for financial restitution or think the offender should do community service work. Offenders, victims and anyone else in the conference may join in the discussion to help forge an agreement acceptable to both offenders and victims. The possible outcomes are as varied as the people who attend the conference.

Often the families of the offenders urge the harshest consequences to demonstrate to the victims and their supporters the shame they feel about their loved ones' wrongdoing. Victims are often remarkably generous. Having had an opportunity to vent their anger and have a say in the outcome, victims frequently feel sorry for those offenders who demonstrate genuine shame and remorse.

When an agreement has been reached, put into writing and signed by all parties, offenders may now alleviate their shame. By apologizing and making amends, by paying restitution and carrying out the other provisions of the plan, offenders can help repair the harm they have caused and be reintegrated back into the community.

After the conference, the facilitator invites all of the participants to have refreshments while the contract is being signed, copied and distributed. During this informal "breaking of bread" the participants begin the process of reintegration so that both offenders and victims can eventually shed their "offender" and "victim" identities and go on with their lives.

When I first heard Terry O'Connell, restorative conferences were being used largely as a diversion from the criminal justice system, not with serious crimes of violence. Few of us then realized how the uses for conferencing would grow. Conferences would eventually be convened after the courts had already dealt with more serious offenses as an opportunity for victims and their families to deal with their feelings and achieve healing. We could not predict that conferencing would be employed beyond schools and the juvenile justice system to respond to adult offenses or offenses in the workplace. We did not envision conferences in churches and camps and youth agencies and with parole violations and in prisons, in short, wherever wrongdoing needed to be addressed. Back then we were just learning the basics.

As I listened to O'Connell, I appreciated his explanation of conferencing because it helped me understand how the process worked. I had difficulty understanding his strong Australian accent and missed some of what he said, but found Terry to be humorous and charismatic. I certainly understood him on an emotional level and was ready to make conferencing happen where I worked and lived.

4

Australia

I felt I had found what I had been seeking since the Uncle Marty Sneaker Barn burglary hearing—a response to crime that meets the needs of victims and others who have been most affected by the offense. I imagined that we could use restorative conferences in our own organization's schools and group homes. I wanted to encourage public schools and police to use conferences with school misconduct and juvenile offenses. I didn't know how I was going to get in touch with Terry O'Connell, who would be traveling for months on his Winston Churchill Fellowship. I had encountered an exciting possibility, but I needed to know more.

My wife, Susan, who helped me initiate the Community Service Foundation, was long accustomed to my outbursts of enthusiasm, so she was not too surprised when I came home that afternoon proclaiming that I had to go to Australia. She listened intently while I explained the restorative conference process and told her a couple of conference stories. She, too, liked the concept and recognized its merit.

A few days later *The Philadelphia Inquirer* covered Terry O'Connell making a similar presentation to the Philadelphia police.

The article's appearance on the front page of the Sunday edition of a major urban newspaper confirmed my strong feelings about the potential of conferencing.

Despite the media attention, Susan and I realized what an arduous task it would be to make conferencing happen beyond the boundaries of our own organization. People would have to change their way of responding to wrongdoing and adopt a whole new perception of justice.

For a few days I thought about my desire to bring conferencing to North America and the implications of that decision. That year I had finally normalized my life, after more than a decade and a half of working evenings and weekends to build the Community Service Foundation. I had recently hired a full-time administrator and was just getting used to the luxury of "free time."

Susan and I had planned a short vacation traveling through northern Pennsylvania. Before we left home, I mailed a letter to Donald Nathanson, the Philadelphia psychiatrist and author who served as the introductory speaker for Terry O'Connell at the luncheon and whose writings helped explain why conferencing worked so well. In my letter I introduced myself to Nathanson, explained that I was thinking about how conferencing might be developed in North America and asked how I might get in touch with O'Connell or his colleagues in Australia.

Our trip through Pennsylvania afforded us time to ponder the road ahead. Susan and I understood that bringing conferencing to North America was more than a day job. If I made the commitment, while Susan continued to supervise our schools, I would have to throw myself passionately into this new effort, working many evenings and weekends again, until the project achieved maturity and viability.

Shortly after we returned from our vacation I received a phone call from Nathanson inviting us to meet with him. He had contacted the Australians by e-mail. They were interested in what I had to say.

Susan and I went to Nathanson's home. He had done some checking on us and our Community Service Foundation, saving us the task of establishing our credibility. He was already aware of our agency's good reputation and my earlier role as one of the cofounders and coauthors of TOUGHLOVE, a national program that helps parents cope with acting-out teen-agers and young adults.

I described my vision of a nonprofit educational program that would develop high-quality trainings and educational materials to foster restorative conferencing throughout North America. Nathanson responded favorably and offered to recommend us to his Australian friends.

Nathanson gave me the e-mail address of a young academician named David Moore who, while at Charles Sturt University in Wagga Wagga, had collaborated with Terry O'Connell. Moore made the original contact with Nathanson because he felt that Don's book *Shame and Pride* helped explain the dynamics of conferencing.

David was invaluable in filling the gaps in my understanding of conferencing. We struck up a vigorous e-mail correspondence. He also sent me copies of several excellent articles about conferencing that he had written for academic publications. By the end of August I was thoroughly convinced that conferencing was all that I had hoped. I began making arrangements for my visit to Australia. My plans became increasingly elaborate and expensive. Initially I intended to talk to Australian police officers and educators who had facilitated restorative conferences and victims, offenders and their families. I hoped that I might even get an opportunity to observe an actual conference. By the time I left for Australia in November I had secured approval from our Community Service Foundation's board of directors to hire a video crew to travel with me and gather footage for a documentary on conferencing.

Arrangements were made with Terry O'Connell and his colleagues for us to videotape interviews with school, police, court and government officials, as well as conference facilitators and victims, offenders, family and friends who had participated in restorative conferences.

What I heard from the conference facilitators and participants themselves further reassured me that conferencing was a practical and reliable approach to addressing incidents of school misconduct and juvenile crime. Here are some of their stories.

Schoolyard Bullies

One Sunday Patrick was playing wall ball in the schoolyard with a friend. He hit his ball over the wall and it landed where several boys were playing basketball. They threw his ball into an adjacent fenced area instead of returning it. When Patrick retrieved his ball, they took it from him and threw it away again. Then they started punching and kicking him. The three assailants bullied him and drove him from the schoolyard, and then repeatedly kicked and hit him as they followed him almost to his home.

According to his mother, Patrick phoned her at work and was in "an incredibly distressed state." She was, of course, angry and upset, but as a professional youth worker she had an unusual perspective, often counseling boys very much like the bullies who battered her son. Her son was afraid of his assailants. He did not even want to tell anyone. But she could not abide simply ignoring the event. When she called the school the next day and the deputy principal suggested convening a restorative conference as a way of dealing with the assault, she was receptive. The conference seemed to her to be a good way to address the bullying.

The conference took place a few days later. It included the three offenders, their parents, Patrick and his mother and older sister. The conference began, as they always do, with the facilitator, in this case the guidance officer, reminding everyone that the conference was voluntary and that participants could leave at any time. She said this conference was not only an alternative to school disciplinary action, but, with the understanding of the local police, also an alternative to prosecution in juvenile court.

Each of the offenders and Patrick individually told what happened. For the offenders' parents, the description of the attack was sobering. Their boys had not only teased and bullied a schoolmate but had abused him in a way that could have caused serious injury. Everyone at the conference had an opportunity to speak about how the incident had affected them. After the agreement had largely been concluded with some very strong consequences for the offenders, and the conference seemed to be coming to a close, Patrick, who had said very little previously, indicated that he wished to speak. He sat up taller than he had been and raised his eyes from looking at the floor. "This is not easy for me," he said, "But I feel like what you are asking these boys to do is not fair. And I would like to see it changed, and this is how I would like to see it changed." He proceeded to reduce or eliminate the harshest aspects of the agreement. The rest of the group, much surprised by his sudden assertiveness, did not argue with his views and the agreement was finalized as he had requested.

In the informal period after the conference, while the contracts were being written and signed, each of the young perpetrators went over to Patrick, apologized to him and shook his hand. His mother described the apology by each of the boys as "very legitimate." She said, "It wasn't posed and it wasn't artificial. It was very real and very strong." She further indicated that her son was "able to go back to school and feel safe."

When I interviewed her for our video production, she summarized her view of the conference process: "If these young people had been charged by the law and gone through the process of juvenile court and those sorts of processes, I don't have any doubt that it would have perpetuated the process of aggression within them. I don't have any doubt that it would have perpetuated the feelings and behavior of victimization on the part of my son."

Patrick's older sister had been skeptical before the conference. "I was quite surprised actually," she said. "It really was a good way to solve the problems between people. And the kids, as far as I know, the boys that attacked my brother, they treat him a lot nicer now. They're friends with him and talk to him and stuff. It was really good."

The Egging

The day her friends threw eggs at her house, 17-year-old Alice moved out of her parents' home and in with her boyfriend's family. The egging, in addition to her many previous difficulties with her parents, brought their relationship to the boiling point. They told her to leave.

Although Alice herself had participated in the egging of other people's houses, when she learned that Helen, a longtime girlfriend, had been among those who egged her parents' home, she was enraged. Mutual friends tried to cool her down, but she refused to listen. Walking down the street with her boyfriend's little sister, Alice encountered Helen. Without waiting for explanations she punched Helen, knocking her to the ground. Helen's parents insisted on bringing charges for assault. The police sergeant handling the case decided to offer a restorative conference as a way of handling the incident, and everyone agreed to participate.

Since Alice was no longer living with her parents, they did not attend the conference. Instead she was supported by her boyfriend's mother and the little sister who had been with her at the time of the assault. Helen was there with her parents. A mutual friend of Alice and Helen attended as well.

At the beginning of the conference Alice apologized to Helen for hitting her, but her grasp of the implications of what she had done was limited. Not until everyone had shared how the assault affected them did Alice really begin to see the extent to which her violence had harmed other people. When the conference facilitator asked the boyfriend's little sister how the incident had affected her, tears came to her eyes, and she said that she had been very frightened and had cried. For Alice, that was the most poignant moment of the conference.

When Helen's angry parents heard Alice talk about her conflict with her parents and realized that she had been put out of her home after their daughter had thrown eggs at the house, they also became more understanding. Not that they felt that Alice was justified in assaulting their daughter, but they saw more clearly how the turmoil in her life had contributed to the event.

The mutual friend told the offender how angry and shocked she was. She pointed out that Alice had been part of egging other people's houses and no one had hit her. She also expressed regret that their group of friends had been torn apart by the assault.

Once the group turned to repairing the harm, they quickly reached an agreement that included a formal apology. This time Alice apologized to Helen and Helen's parents with a much deeper understanding of how many people had been adversely affected by her act of violence.

I interviewed the mutual friend who had attended in support of both victim and offender. She was delighted that her friends were back on good terms because of the conference. "I was amazed," she said, "I thought it was really good that a policeman would actually sit down and try to work things out in that perspective instead of just paperwork, filing and OK, your court date's this day. I thought this was good, that it will work, and it did work."

Alice described to me her reaction to her boyfriend's little sister in the conference. "I felt bad," she said. "I made her cry. I felt low, ashamed that I'd done it in front of her, and that she'd seen me do it. That maybe she'll go out and hit one of her friends or something. I felt like a bad example."

Victim Generosity

As I interviewed the Australian conference participants, I began to realize that the conference process dramatically transforms the victims' perspective. If they have an opportunity to express their feelings and have those feelings acknowledged by others, especially the offenders, they often put aside their own anger and hurt and are remarkably forgiving.

I was particularly struck by the generosity of Mary, a woman who had her car vandalized. Only six weeks before, her car had been stolen from the same parking lot. After waiting a long time for her insurance company to pay her, her new car was now damaged by three boys who wedged a fire hose in the exhaust pipe and turned the water on full blast. They also let the air out of all four tires.

The conference was convened with the three offenders. Two of the boys were brothers and came to the conference with their parents. The third boy, Will, came with his mother. Mary came by herself, although she had been encouraged to bring supporters. Apparently her husband had to be at work.

The boys began by explaining that two of them were supposed to be in school and the older brother was supposed to be looking for a job. They were wandering around town, saw the car in the parking lot next to the fire hose and started fooling around with it. One thing led to another.

Mary was angry when the conference began, but she seemed relieved to learn that her car was selected at random because it was in the wrong place at the wrong time, not because it was hers. Initially she may have feared that the vandalism was related to the car theft six weeks before. She explained how she heard that her car had been damaged, how her husband started the car and how relieved he was that more water did not get into the engine and cause substantial damage. He was eventually able to start the car after draining the oil and replacing some parts. At one point in telling the story Mary began to cry.

The parents of the two boys and Will's mother were effusive in their apologies. Then both of the mothers also began to cry, insisting that they had not raised their children to behave like this.

In the agreement phase of the conference, everyone agreed that the boys themselves should pay the costs. At this point Mary said that she didn't care if they paid a little every week, but the parents insisted that they should pay right away, that they had enough money. The two brothers apologized and paid. Will remained conspicuously silent and seemed very reluctant to pay up. He had yet to take any responsibility or express any remorse. He seemed not to care and was annoyed that he had to be at the conference. On a couple of occasions during the conference he even asked the police officer when he could leave.

In frustration his mother began to cry again. She explained that Will's father was in jail for beating her up. She said that she had been having trouble getting him to do what he was supposed to do. But eventually Will agreed and paid his share of the money also.

The conference ended and during the informal phase, the two brothers apologized again and the two mothers hugged and kissed Mary, repeatedly apologizing for what their children had done. The father also expressed his deep disappointment with his sons.

The police officer took Will and his mother aside and recommended a counseling agency that might help the two of them deal with the tough times they were going through. Will did not object.

When I interviewed Mary I asked her why she was so willing to have the boys pay a little at a time, despite the fact that she had been so inconvenienced and wronged. She said to me, "I just felt sort of guilty."

I must have shown some surprise on my face because she quickly added, "Well, not guilty. I just sort of felt sorry for them, more than anything. I thought they were sorry, but I didn't expect them to pay me up front. But it was the parents that actually wanted them to pay. The most important thing that came out of the conference is that they came, and they were sorry for what they had done, and they apologized. And they apologized quite a few times. And they gave the money, so I was happy."

Mary's generosity is more the rule than the exception. Contrary to the popular view, victims do not want revenge. If offenders show genuine remorse and agree to right the wrong, most victims are easily satisfied. More than anything, victims want to feel better.

Bearded Dragon

Sometimes conferences don't go smoothly. That usually has something to do with a flaw in preparation for the conference. Ideally the conference facilitator visits or phones every individual who will be attending. When this doesn't happen, problems may arise. In this story, which involved the killing of a wild animal on school grounds, the parents of one of the two offenders came without understanding the reason for the conference.

Bob and Allen tortured a "bearded dragon," a relatively scarce species of lizard, during the school day. Other students who observed the cruelty and ultimately the killing of the animal were very upset. After several students went to teachers and the school administration, the school decided to hold a restorative conference to deal with the incident.

The conference facilitator scrambled to invite everyone but had not been able to reach Allen's parents, nor had he prepared Allen for the conference by talking to him about what he had done. Allen had admitted to his parents that he had killed the bearded dragon, but claimed it was done as an act of mercy after his friend Bob had tortured it. So Allen's parents entered the conference harboring the feeling that their son had been unjustly accused.

Besides the two boys and their parents, the conference was attended by concerned students, some of their parents and several faculty members. The normal conference routine was upset by Allen's parents, who protested the accusations against their son and the need for the conference itself. The facilitator realized his mistake in not clarifying Allen's situation beforehand but decided to proceed anyway.

The offenders' parents heard their sons describe what they had done and then heard other students and the teachers speak, in very emotional terms, about how that kind of cruelty had affected them. A few of the students cried. Some teachers spoke about the growing effort on the part of the school to help protect the wildlife in the vicinity of the school.

Both Bob's and Allen's parents were moved by the sincerity and emotionality of the students and faculty. They began to recognize that what their boys had done was not just a boyish prank, but an affront to the sensibilities of many well-meaning people who wanted to protect increasingly threatened wildlife and the environment in general.

By the end of the conference the adversarial tone that began the conference had completely subsided. The two boys expressed their regret and offered to help with a tree-planting project on the school grounds as a way of demonstrating their sincerity. The anger of the other students, and the faculty disappeared in light of the boys' change in attitude.

Despite faulty preparation for this conference, the process proved robust enough to allow a good outcome. Bob and Allen were forgiven by their fellow students, and the incident raised the environmental consciousness of the entire school community.

No Big Deal

We often judge the emotional impact of a crime by the severity of the offense, but lesser crimes often wreak havoc in people's lives, not because of physical harm but because the crime disrupts their feelings of safety and normality.

Terry O'Connell told me a story while I was in Australia about the theft of a motor bike from the veranda of a suburban home. No big deal. Just a motor bike, not much expense, no violence. The family consisted of a mom and dad and four little girls who ranged in age from 4 to 12 years old.

Terry "rang" the mother on the telephone and asked if she wanted to participate in a restorative conference with the two teenage boys who had been apprehended and had admitted the offense. "No, we would be too terrified," she said. "I'm going to get counselors. My family has been severely traumatized."

Terry responded sympathetically. He asked if he could come and speak to the family personally, to explain how the conference might address that fear and trauma. The mother agreed, and after his visit the family eventually agreed to participate in a conference.

In the conference, the mother spoke emotionally to the boys, as did the oldest sister. Both spoke in general terms about how the theft had traumatized the younger sisters. Although they talked only in general terms in the conference, Terry later learned that the youngest sister, after the incident, started wetting her bed. Still another insisted on sleeping with her parents. The second oldest sister wouldn't go out on the back veranda after dark.

Because the motor bike was recovered, there was no financial restitution involved. The agreement focused on apologies and some community service work.

After the conference ended and the offenders left, O'Connell chatted with the family. The mother assured him that the conference had brought her family closure. She said that she had no idea how they would have effectively dealt with the aftermath of this event without the conference. The 12-year-old began to cry, with her younger sisters watching her. "I felt really sorry for those two boys," she exclaimed. "They're just like the boys down the road." For she and her sisters the face-to-face meeting with the boys made the offenders real and normal, removing the fear from their nights.

When Terry followed up a week later, the mother said that the conference had been a fabulous experience for the family. The girls had not stopped talking about it. The issues of trauma had not surfaced again and the family's life had returned to normal.

When I interviewed John Braithwaite, the well-known Australian criminologist, whose book *Crime, Shame and Reintegration* provides a sociological explanation for why conferencing is so effective, he told me about a conference he had observed. His story further illustrates why we cannot assume that a lesser crime has only a modest impact on victims.

An elderly woman's pension check was stolen from her mailbox by a teen-age girl. At the outset of the restorative conference it became clear that the youth had assumed that the woman was in a much better financial position than she actually was and would not really miss the money.

But the girl's eyes grew wider as the woman explained that the pension check was her primary source of income. After the theft occurred she was so frightened that she spent hundreds of dollars from her modest savings to put special locks and security bolts on all of her doors and windows. And so did the other elderly woman living next to her.

The young girl was astonished by the fear and expense she had caused by her seemingly petty theft. Had this offender been prosecuted through the courts without a restorative conference, she would never have achieved this realization.

CHAPTER 5

Restorative Justice

I said goodbye to most of my Australian friends at a barbecue in Terry O'Connell's backyard and parted company with the video crew. After nine hectic days of non-stop travel and videotaping, I had seen little of Australia except police stations, high schools and a dead kangaroo by the side of the highway, although I did meet a lot of lovely people.

As I made the long trip back to Philadelphia, I began to face the magnitude of the project I had undertaken: to implement restorative conferencing throughout North America. What had I been thinking? How audacious. How grandiose. How overwhelming.

Returning home in time for Thanksgiving gave me a chance to recover from extreme jet lag, switching from day to night and summer to winter, before resuming work. Then I began to implement what we had decided to call the Real Justice program.

My first priority was to organize a training for the staff of our own organization, Community Service Foundation. I decided to hold two trainings, one before a weekend and one after the weekend, so that we could send half our staff one week and half the next. The Australians and I had tentatively planned a training for March

1995, which left me about four months to recruit enough paid trainees to share the costs of this expensive undertaking.

I made my first attempt at promoting Real Justice in early December, inviting a group of educators, police and probation officers to see some clips from the interviews we had videotaped in Australia. I discovered then something I would find in each one of the hundreds of presentations I would make over the next few years: There is at least one person in each group who makes the same strong intuitive connection that I did and comes away with an enthusiastic interest in finding out more about conferencing. Although I also encountered cautious skeptics, I almost never experienced strong opposition because there is something about conferencing that simply makes sense, even if one needs further convincing.

As I began my efforts, I was largely unaware of a significant factor working in my favor. Although my own instincts had independently led me to pursue conferencing, my inclination was consistent with a growing interest in North America in a concept called "restorative justice."

Although I was vaguely familiar with the term, I began to gain a deeper understanding of the concept when I went to Minnesota in January 1995 to videotape some interviews with a police department that was doing a modified version of the conferencing process developed in Wagga Wagga.

On the same trip, at the urging of Terry O'Connell, I visited with Kay Pranis, the restorative justice planner for the Minnesota Department of Corrections. I have been forever thankful for his recommendation. Kay has consistently guided and challenged me toward a deeper understanding of the significance of conferencing and its implications within the larger context of restorative justice.

Kay spent a Sunday with me, introducing me to Mark Umbreit, a leading proponent of victim-offender mediation, and showing me a videotape that acquainted me with Howard Zehr, whose book *Changing Lenses* is one of the seminal works and most helpful explanations of restorative justice available.

Zehr's background includes his Mennonite heritage of peacemaking, direct experience with offenders and their victims and an active interest in photography, which influenced his book's title. In *Changing Lenses* he points out that we currently look at justice through a "retributive" lens, viewing crime as an offense against the state that requires punishment. He suggests that we look at justice through a "restorative" lens, recognizing that a crime is actually committed against people and that the focus of justice should be on restoration of the victims' well-being.

Restorative conferencing represents the latter perspective, where we emphasize repairing the harm by addressing the emotional and material needs of victims. Conferencing includes as participants the community defined by the offense, which David Moore, the Australian academician, has defined as the "micro-community": the victim, the offender and their respective family and friends. I came to the realization that although victim-offender mediation was the dominant model of restorative justice practice at the time, conferencing more adequately matches the ideal expressed by Zehr because it includes not only the victim and offender but also the family and friends of both. Real Justice also goes beyond the criminal justice system to deal with wrongdoing in schools, workplaces, anywhere that a more effective response would be useful—presumably everywhere.

I felt affirmed in advocating restorative conferencing and appreciated Zehr's articulate explanation of a new way of looking at justice. I especially valued his descriptive contrast and comparison of retributive and restorative justice, which I have adapted slightly and expressed below as the ten differences between Real Justice or restorative justice and our current criminal justice systems or school disciplinary systems.

1. In our current systems an offense is defined as a violation against the system, as a crime against the state. In Real Justice or restorative justice, an offense is defined as the harm that is done to a person or the community.

2. In our current systems the focus is on establishing blame and guilt. In Real Justice the focus is on solving problems, on how to repair the harm.

3. In our current systems the victim is largely ignored. In Real Justice the victim's rights and needs are fully recognized.

4. In our current systems the offender is passive, but in Real Justice the offender is encouraged to take responsibility.

5. Currently we define accountability as punishment. Real Justice defines accountability as demonstrating empathy and helping to repair harm.

6. In our current response to an offense we focus on the offender's past behavior, but in Real Justice we focus on the harmful consequences of the offender's behavior.

7. Under our current systems the stigma of crime is largely unremovable, but in Real Justice the stigma of crime is removable through appropriate actions by the offender.

8. Currently there is little encouragement for repentance, but in Real Justice repentance is encouraged and forgiveness is possible.

9. Our current systems depend on professionals for justice. Real Justice relies instead on the direct involvement of those who have been affected.

10. Our current system is strictly rational, but Real Justice allows and encourages the free expression of emotion.

Derived from the ancient tradition of the Maori, incorporated into New Zealand law and adapted by an Australian police officer, Real Justice conferencing began in North America in late 1994 and coincided with the restorative justice movement, an ongoing effort to reform our current criminal justice system.

CHAPTER 6

Sowing the Seeds

In March 1995, Terry O'Connell and four other Australians arrived to lead the two trainings organized by Real Justice in Pennsylvania. The twelve days they stayed with our family and next door at my sister Rebecca's home were a constant buzz of activity, both exciting and exhausting. My sons Ben and Josh, one just finished with college and the other awaiting his stint in the Peace Corps, chauffeured the Australians and others from place to place. My wife, Susan, and I attended to meals and kept things organized while our 12-year-old daughter Katie helped where she could.

Ever since I heard Terry O'Connell speak and especially since I returned from my trip, we anticipated with growing enthusiasm the arrival of the trainers who would help us launch the Real Justice program in North America.

In the four months since I visited Australia we had assembled over 150 trainees: educators, youth counselors, police, probation officers and others from Pennsylvania, Minnesota, Vermont, Ontario and as far away as Alabama. In Minnesota Kay Pranis had recruited the largest out-of-town contingent. Canadians, having encountered Terry O'Connell and David Moore on their earlier visits to North America, comprised the next largest group.

Nishnawbe-Aski Legal Services, which serves about 50 remote First Nations (in the U.S. we say Native American) communities near Thunder Bay, Ontario, sent a half dozen representatives. Their purpose was to acquaint some of the young leaders of these Cree and Ojibwa villages with an approach to justice similar to the way First Nations people responded to wrongdoing for centuries before they were forced to abandon their practices by the Canadian government. Now, in an era when First Nations people are gaining greater autonomy, restorative conferencing offers a practical model for restoring a more traditional approach to justice.

Both trainings went well. Many of the trainees, including our own staff, had been sent by their agencies and were skeptical at first, but they responded to the obvious intelligence, passion and commitment of the Australian trainers. In the end most of the trainees were enthusiastic and made commitments to try conferencing in their own settings.

Seeing My First Conference

While the Australians were here for the training, I finally got the opportunity to see my first restorative conference. My previous impressions of conferencing had relied on written accounts or my interviews with conference participants in Australia. Three months before the first Real Justice training three youths had thrown "Molotov cocktails" into a family's suburban home in the middle of the night. Only smoke detectors saved the lives of the father, mother and their 17-year-old daughter and 12-year-old son, sleeping on the second floor. They were awakened just before all the oxygen was consumed by the flames on the first floor. They escaped with their lives, but the entire family was traumatized, especially Tom, the 12-year-old son.

The young offenders were apprehended and admitted their guilt, but the arson victims remained in shock and disarray. They were living in temporary quarters and relying on donations of clothing, food and other support from neighbors and relatives. They were further demoralized when the offenders went through a court hearing to determine whether they should be certified as adults rather than be dealt with by the juvenile justice system. The victims had to listen as witness after witness, in an effort to keep the teen-agers from being sent to adult prison, told the judge how good the offenders really were. The victims also heard the suggestion that a racial slur by their daughter against one of the offenders had provoked the incident.

The victims could not respond to the allegations in that setting. They had no opportunity to ask the offenders questions, challenge how an alleged racial slur might have justified such a violent response or present their own story. They could only listen and see the allegations and the outcome repeated in the newspapers the next day. The three offenders were not dealt with as adults but sent to a secure juvenile treatment facility.

A forensic psychologist suggested that a restorative conference would benefit the victims, the offenders, their friends and families and the local community, which was still shocked and unresolved. The psychologist was aware that the pioneer of Australian conferencing, Terry O'Connell, was going to be visiting the U.S. to conduct trainings and felt that his visit offered an opportunity for an experienced conference facilitator to bring healing to all those who had been affected by the crime. Terry agreed to facilitate the conference.

Because the conference is voluntary for both offenders and victims, O'Connell went through the process of inviting victims and offenders to participate. He also met with and reassured the court victim-witness coordinator and several juvenile probation officers, who were understandably worried that the conference might cause more harm than good. They were especially concerned that the unresolved issue of the racial slur would cause the conference to overheat and boil. O'Connell assured them that it would not.

As the two groups, the offenders and their family and friends and the victims and their family and friends, arrived, O'Connell directed them to two separate rooms. After seating arrangements were explained and some questions and concerns were addressed, the 30 participants entered the conference room and took their seats. The participants sat in a circle. Observers, like myself, sat out of the circle and some distance from the group.

O'Connell explained, stating the standard preamble in the script used for all restorative conferences, that the purpose of the conference was to find out how the incident had affected everyone and how to repair the harm caused by the young offenders' actions. To his immediate left sat the 12-year-old victim, Tom, facing away from the rest of the circle with an upraised arm shielding himself from any view of the offenders. Of the victim's family, he was the one most visibly traumatized by the experience.

The group was then guided through the process. Initially the offenders were asked individually to describe the events leading up to the incident, the incident itself, what they were thinking about at the time and what they thought about afterward. Although some of the observers had previously wondered if it would be more empowering to allow the victims to speak first, the process seemed to work well with the young offenders admitting to their misdeeds, in their own words, right at the outset.

Next the victims spoke, expressing their outrage at what had been done to them. They described how they had lost everything in the fire, were living in turmoil without a home and had their lives changed forever. The mother insisted that the offenders would have to reassure her 12-year-old son that they would never hurt him again.

After all of the victims' relatives and friends expressed their feelings, Tom, who had initially refused to speak and who would not even face the circle, now turned and spoke directly to the offenders with emotional eloquence. Pouring out his anger and fear, he told the offenders that he could barely sleep, every sound startled him, every siren unnerved him, that he could hardly concentrate, and that he lived in fear that they would hurt him again. Tom said that he found himself always grumpy, preoccupied with his fears and unable to do or accomplish anything. He said that he only came to the conference because the rest of his family was coming.

The offenders sat with their heads bowed. Although some observers later commented that they expected the offenders to cry and show more emotion, those who are more familiar with the process realize that some people are not given to emotional displays. They advise observers to watch for more universal expressions of shame such as "showing the victim the top of their heads" or bowing in shame.

After the victims and their friends and family finished speaking, Terry shifted the focus to the family and friends of the young offenders. They spoke about how sorry they felt about what had happened and said that they could not understand how the three boys had done what they had done. The offenders continued to sit with their heads bowed.

O'Connell then asked the group what could be done to repair the harm. He asked the victims what they expected from the two offenders. One of the victims' friends suggested an apology as a start, and the offenders apologized. The injured mother demanded that the three offenders assure Tom that they would never do anything like this again, which they readily did. They also said that they wished they could take back what they had done. The victim's father said that all he wanted was some relief from the trauma they had endured and that he felt the conference itself was helpful.

In this final phase of the conference it became clear that the two sides had become a circle, that the two groups had become one community. For example, a teen-age friend of one of the offenders, expressing concern about the effect all the publicity had had on the victimized family, suggested that he and the daughter collaborate on an article for the school newspaper talking about how life had been for the victim family since the incident. Everyone agreed.

The alleged racial slur, which several participants had mentioned, failed to emerge as an issue in the conference, as some had feared beforehand. One of the conference participants said to the offenders, "I hope that you have learned from this experience that life isn't always fair, but that taking revenge doesn't help at all."

The father of one of the offenders reassured the victims: "We are very, very sorry."

The daughter spoke of her family's determination to overcome this setback in their lives and return to a normal life. She also initiated a series of "thank yous" from participants to the facilitator, Terry O'Connell, for having convened the conference.

Immediately after the conference, members of the victims' and offenders' groups approached each other. There was animated conversation, even joking. Knowledgeable observers noted that the conference helped alleviate post-traumatic stress caused by the crime, particularly for 12-year-old victim Tom. He now stood strong and erect, fully engaged in conversation, a smile on his face.

The arson conference allowed me to experience firsthand the power of conferencing. For anger and anxiety of such intensity to give way to smiles and relief was a remarkable transformation. The victims eventually returned to their renovated home, and the offenders spent almost two years in juvenile treatment facilities and group homes. Neither victims nor offenders waltzed off into the sunset. A singular event cannot eliminate all the problems related to a crime. Yet the conference was healing for individuals and the community, with a far better result than the court process.

After experiencing the arson conference and both trainings, I was more committed than ever to fostering the spread of conferencing. The seeds had been carried from Australia and planted in the fertile soil of North America. I had high hopes that conferencing would take root and start to grow.

CHAPTER 7

North American Stories

After the first Real Justice trainings, North American trainees began to conduct conferences. Every week we heard from enthusiastic conference facilitators—a police officer, educator or juvenile probation officer who had successfully convened a restorative conference.

Cannonball Run

Early one morning, a few weeks after the Australians conducted the first Real Justice trainings, I received a phone call from an assistant principal who wanted to know if we had any suggestions for convening a restorative conference with 75 participants—which he planned to hold that night. I lacked the experience to answer his questions, but early morning in Pennsylvania was late evening in Australia, so I called Marg Thorsborne, a guidance officer in Queensland who had run an unusually large conference for a group of students who had slaughtered birds in a nature reserve.

With both the assistant principal and myself on the telephone line, she suggested that the chairs be configured in curved rows facing each other. The usual circular arrangement would place everyone too far from each other, and the circle itself would be far too large.

She also warned that the conference would run far longer than the usual hour or so because many people would want a chance to talk. She was pleased to hear that a police officer who had also been trained in conferencing would help manage the event, ushering people into the room and attending to other details while the assistant principal facilitated the conference itself. Because of the extended time that people would be there, she recommended having plenty of snacks and beverages available so that individuals could take short refreshment breaks while the conference proceeded.

After we ended our telephone connection to Australia the assistant principal explained that for several years a group of juniors and seniors had been staging an annual "Cannonball Run," a high-speed auto race on public roads. The race was named after an old Burt Reynolds movie and was held on the day of the high school senior awards assembly. The assistant principal and local police had tried to prevent this year's race, but several students had managed to either sneak off school grounds or simply had not come to school that day. Speeding through small towns on rural roads, they had avoided the police until one of the racers hit another car. The occupants of the car that had been struck were not seriously injured but were quite shaken by the crash.

With several of the race participants in custody, the police learned the names of all of the participants. Recently trained in restorative conferencing, the assistant principal and juvenile officer agreed that the incident would be perfect for a conference. They decided to convene the conference in the town where the accident had occurred for the convenience of the accident victims and other irate citizens who had also been affected. Seventeen students, their parents and some of their siblings brought the attendance to the projected total of around 75.

The conference lasted five hours. First each student told his part in the race. Although they expressed remorse, when they heard from the accident victims and others who had been affected by the race, they began to realize the serious consequences of their behavior. They had terrified a large number of people.

In telling me about the conference the assistant principal described how the parents, sitting in rows behind their sons, became increasingly upset and ashamed. Each boy would occasionally look back to try to catch a glimpse of his parents' reactions as the conference proceeded. Those parents whose sons had minimized the nature of the race, who were only cautiously cooperative or who had some objection to the conference location, miles from their home community, now fully appreciated the harm their sons had done to others and the risks that the boys themselves had taken. When the parents had the opportunity to speak they apologized profusely to the victims of the Cannonball Run and strongly supported whatever consequences the group would recommend.

Because of the length of the conference, some participants became restless. The police officer chatted with people as they visited the refreshment table, encouraging them to see the conference through. Almost everyone stayed for the full five hours. In the agreement phase of the conference the suggestions were written on a large flip chart and then edited down into an acceptable plan. When the conference ended, most people stayed and socialized while each conference participant signed the agreement displayed on the flip chart.

The most important item in the agreement was a promise by the students to help prevent another Cannonball Run in the future. Seniors agreed to advise younger students against continuing the dangerous tradition and juniors agreed to do the same, especially as seniors the following year.

Another significant development came as a result of the candid discussion fostered by the conference. The Cannonball Run was perceived as a symbolic protest by many youths, who resented the compulsory nature of the awards assembly, in which some students received awards while the rest of the student body was required to attend. The school decided to change its awards ceremony to an evening event for the award recipients, their families and any of their fellow students who chose to attend.

There has not been another Cannonball Run.

Two-Timer

Roger, a student at an alternative school, had been driving everyone crazy with his disruptive behavior. The school typically asks its students to actively support the counselors and teachers in maintaining decorum. After months of both students and staff confronting this youth on his inappropriate actions and encouraging him to make changes, the staff had reached their limit.

Having just attended the Real Justice training, the school staff proposed to conduct a restorative conference to deal with Roger's latest classroom disruption. They limited it to the "last incident" because the staff had learned that a conference should focus on a single event. The incident might involve several elements, like someone burglarizing three houses on a single night, but should stay within a narrow time frame. Limiting the conference to one incident keeps the process focused and manageable. Although conference participants will bring up other incidents and behaviors in the normal course of expressing their feelings and talking about what happened, the facilitator should not interrupt unless they wander too far afield. If the discussion does drift, the conference facilitator merely refocuses by gently reminding the group about the incident that brought them together and the goal of repairing the harm caused by that specific event.

In deciding who will run the conference, potential facilitators must recognize when their feelings might interfere with the process and should find another trained facilitator to convene the conference. In this case the staff invited a counselor from another school to act as the facilitator. Staff members realized that they felt victimized by Roger's behavior and wanted the opportunity to express how they were affected by him.

The facilitator invited Roger's father, who had frequently been involved in telephone calls and meetings about his son, and his mother, who was recovering from an automobile accident and had not been previously involved. When asked to nominate other supporters, Roger named several of the students who attended school with him.

The conference was convened in the evening. Roger began by acknowledging his responsibility for the recent classroom disruption. The school teachers and counselors expressed how angry and frustrated they were with him. His mother was especially emotional. She brought everyone to the brink of tears as her emotion resonated around the room. His father also expressed feelings, but Roger was particularly touched by fellow students, who said that they were afraid he was going to be discharged from the school and that they would miss him.

Roger expressed remorse and was extremely motivated in the agreement phase of the conference, coming up with all sorts of practical suggestions for how he could do things differently in the future. For example, he committed to appropriately make statements or ask questions at least three times in each of his history and English classes.

In the days and weeks following the conference, he kept his commitment. Although he occasionally lapsed into old annoying behaviors, Roger responded favorably when confronted by his fellow students or program staff members. In general, both students and staff were satisfied that he had made significant changes—until he was involved in a major behavior incident on the school bus.

Roger and a girl who attended his school yelled and cursed at the bus driver when he challenged their misbehavior on the bus. Roger also kicked something on the floor near the driver's seat, which hit the driver's leg.

Given the success of the first conference and the significant changes in behavior that resulted from it, the staff decided to try a conference for the bus incident. This is the first instance I know about in which an offender was conferenced twice. However, when Roger was asked who he wanted to nominate as supporters at the conference, he insisted that this time he didn't want any of his schoolmates present. When pressed for a reason, he admitted that he was too ashamed to have them there.

The most notable moment in the conference came when the bus driver poured out his anger and disgust at Roger and exclaimed that he was so fed up with the kind of abuse he got from kids on the bus that he was going to quit his job. Roger was stunned. He truly had no idea his behavior had had such an adverse impact on the bus driver. His sincere remorse moved the bus driver, who graciously accepted the boy's heartfelt apology.

Most significantly the conference demonstrated the community-building potential of restorative conferences—to create relationships where they did not exist previously. The bus driver and his tormentor became friends, developing a positive relationship in the aftermath of a serious altercation.

The bus driver had no further difficulties with Roger's behavior on the school bus.

No Pinch Hitters

A basic tenet of conference preparation is that the facilitator, not someone else, must contact the participants. Critical to the success of the conference is the rapport that the participants have with the person running it. We were advised by the Australians against letting someone else set up our conference for us, but it was only a matter of time until someone put that advice to the test.

Rachel was asked by a school counselor to convene a conference for a student the counselor particularly liked. He wanted the conference to take place quickly, so instead of waiting for Rachel to contact the participants, he made the phone calls to the participants instead. Rachel knew that she should have called everyone but, feeling the time pressure from the other counselor, agreed to facilitate the conference without talking to any of the participants beforehand.

From the moment Rachel walked into the conference room she knew she was in trouble. She had entered a room full of strangers and felt no connection with any of them. As the conference began, the girl who was the offender did not take appropriate responsibility for her behavior. If Rachel had prepared the offender for the conference, she would have reminded the offender of what she said when they talked privately. But Rachel never had such a conversation with the girl. Participants interrupted each other frequently. When Rachel tried to redirect the conference, people ignored her. The offender's grandfather rambled on aimlessly while others tried to talk. At one point in the conference the offender got up, left the room and then came back again. The conference stumbled its way to some sort of agreement and an unsatisfactory conclusion.

Rachel went home and cried. She later said that the conference had felt like a nightmare, with no way to wake up and escape it. It just went on its own way, having slipped beyond her control.

Rachel fully acknowledged her error. She had allowed the other counselor's agenda to dictate the procedure, rather than follow what she knew to be correct.

The lesson from her unpleasant experience is that successful conferences are based on the relationships established before the conference begins. The bonds built by the facilitator with each phone call and each personal visit to the victim, the offender, each of their family members and each of their friends are pieces of a jigsaw puzzle that come together at the time of the conference. Anyone at the conference who has no connection with the facilitator is like a missing piece. With too many missing pieces the puzzle becomes unrecognizable.

Expectations are established by the preparatory contacts. Each person feels respected and valued as the facilitator asks for his or her voluntary participation, patiently explains the process, answers questions and acknowledges feelings. When the participants come to the conference they return that respect by taking direction from the facilitator, by staying within the bounds that the facilitator has previously outlined.

A conference is a baseball game with no pinch hitters. If you want to facilitate the conference, you have to play the whole game, and the game starts with the conference preparation.

CHAPTER **8**

Free Expression

Until you have seen Real Justice in action you might assume that those who say conferencing "works like magic" are exaggerating. But those of us who have seen a conference transform anger and hostility into cooperation and resolution find ourselves amazed and wondering "Why does it work so well?" According to Silvan Tomkins's affect theory, conferencing works so well because it provides a setting that allows for free expression of emotion, minimizing expression of negative emotions and maximizing expression of positive emotions.

David Moore, Terry O'Connell's colleague, discovered Tomkins's affect theory as it was explained in Donald Nathanson's book *Shame and Pride*. Nathanson, you may recall, introduced O'Connell at the juvenile court luncheon where I first heard Terry speak and is a practicing psychiatrist, lecturer and founder of the Silvan S. Tomkins Institute. Although I found Nathanson very interesting, I did not have direct experience with conferencing and could not then appreciate how affect theory served to explain the phenomenon of conferencing.

Affect Theory

Tomkins identified nine basic "affects," which exist in every human being. The six negative affects are disgust, dissmell (revulsion to offensive odor), anger-rage, distress-anguish, fear-terror and shame-humiliation. Surprise-startle is a neutral affect. Lastly, the two positive affects are interest-excitement and enjoyment-joy (see Figure 1). Tomkins presented most affects as hyphenated word pairs identifying a continuum or range between the least and most intensive expressions of that affect.

These nine affects are inherent in every human being. You can see them most clearly expressed on the faces of babies. Babies everywhere in the world express affects in the same way. Affects evolved as life evolved and are fundamental to our survival. Dissmell (a term coined by Tomkins), for example, is how we react when something smells awful and it keeps us from eating something that might kill us. Fear-terror helps us respond to danger. Anger-rage prepares us to attack. Interest-excitement guides us toward what we need to know.

Unlike babies, adults have learned how to modify facial expressions to mask true feelings. Also, reactions to affects can be changed by experiences. This is what Tomkins called "emotion." Unlike affect, emotions differ between individuals and cultures. Emotion is affect after it has been acted upon by the events of our lives. Nathanson says it nicely: affect is biology, emotion is biography. However, for my purposes in this book, I use the terms affect and emotion interchangeably.

In a restorative conference there is a natural progression from negative emotions to positive emotions, fostered by free expression. When the participants first enter the room, anger, disgust, distress and fear abound. As the offenders and victims relate their experience, offenders and their families feel shame. If offenders accept responsibility and victims feel acknowledged, negative emotions can give way to interest and enjoyment. Sometimes after the conference, there is even excitement and joy.

THE NINE AFFECTS
Figure 1

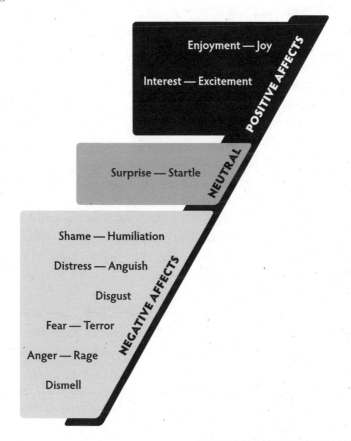

ADAPTED FROM NATHANSON, 1992

People recognize the affects displayed on each other's faces and tend to respond in kind. Tomkins called this "affective resonance" or empathy. The result of affective resonance is that the participants in the conference make the emotional journey together, feeling each other's feelings as they travel from anger and distress and shame to interest and enjoyment. As a conference facilitator, I am always fascinated by the shift toward the positive emotions that usually occurs after the offender has shown genuine remorse and the victim has had an opportunity to express feelings. When discussion turns to repairing the harm, the atmosphere is far more positive than when the conference began.

Ground Rules

The conference provides a safe place for people to freely express their emotions. Sometimes people ask me, "Don't you have to set ground rules so that people won't abuse one another?" Their fear is that emotions will flow too freely. But if the conference facilitator has prepared everyone for the conference properly, the tone is already set for the conference through initial contacts with participants. You have talked with each person individually. You have respectfully explained the purpose of the conference: to find out how people have been affected by the incident and how to repair the harm that it caused. You have emphasized that participation is voluntary and asked for their participation. You have talked in terms of providing support for victims and offenders in a difficult encounter. So you have begun to "set ground rules" with your respectful tone and the voluntary nature of your invitation, without having to verbalize rules.

Compare this approach to how a court system sends written subpoenas or how schools contact the parents of an offending student. The contacts are formal and mandatory. The tone is intimidating. But with a conference, people sense that this is a more positive and respectful way to deal with wrongdoing than any other process they have experienced. That is why they usually agree to come. That is why they stay within the bounds that you have informally set. When the conference begins, as facilitator you reiterate that participation is voluntary and that anyone may leave at any time. A key phrase in the script is, "We are not here to decide if (the offender's name) is a good or bad person." You also repeat the purpose, "To find out how people have been affected by the incident and how to repair the harm that it caused." Although it may seem repetitive, I find that the phrases that define the conference purpose later serve as a useful cue when participants' anger boils over or when they become abusive. In the spirit of Tomkins, I allow them some opportunity to freely express themselves, but then I gently intervene and minimize the negative emotion by repeating the conference purpose. Having heard the conference purpose repeated earlier, people almost always recognize the reminder that they may express only how they have been affected and they stop their abusive verbal attack.

I am certain there are those who are dubious as they read this, questioning why conferences don't slip out of control and perhaps become violent. Because of the facilitator's preparatory effort that does not happen. Those who agree to participate in conferences have voluntarily selected the process, so they are willing to accept the limits of the conference.

Certain Violence

Nonetheless, some conference participants arouse our fears that the worst will happen. A high school principal told me about a conference in which everyone was sure the parents of the student offender and the parents of the student victim would come to blows. Every time the conference facilitator spoke to them they ranted and raved about the other parents, demeaning them, their child and the way they had raised that child, all in the strongest terms. Some of the school faculty began to question the wisdom of the conference and feared that it would deteriorate into a screaming match or violence.

But it did not. The conference began, as all conferences begin, with the offender telling what happened. The victim's parents first heard the acceptance of responsibility by the offender, and then they began to realize that there were important details of the offender's story that differed from their own child's version of events, details that suggested that their own child had some responsibility for the incident. In fact, they found the offender very believable. When the victim and the victim's parents spoke, the offender's parents also realized that they had misunderstood some of the circumstances. When each of the parents talked about how the incident had affected them and admitted having made some assumptions that were not accurate, the other parents recognized that they themselves had acted in the same way. Feelings of anger and mistrust changed to mutual understanding. The principal reported that the parents were so engaged in conversation after the conference that he had to usher them out of the building. He left them standing on the school steps, almost oblivious to his departure.

Hostile Mothers

Although I am certainly not aware of all the conferences that have been convened in the United States and Canada, I am in a position to hear about a great many. The worst of those conferences, in terms of excessive anger, was run by a police officer who found the mothers of the victim and offender to be extremely hostile and uncooperative. The mothers blamed and argued and, unlike most conference participants, interrupted each other and yelled. Finally a senior police officer observing the conference suggested that the conference participants take a brief recess, just to cool things down. While they were in the hall the two mothers discovered that they had gone to the same high school. The coincidence of going to the same school was helpful and the recess itself dramatically emphasized the need for more appropriate behavior. When the conference reconvened it proceeded to a positive conclusion.

Of course, not all conferences run perfectly. Occasionally the offenders do not express remorse or do so only minimally. In those cases, victims at least get the opportunity to express themselves, even though they don't get what they had hoped to get from the offenders. A good conference facilitator prepares victims for that possibility. Nonetheless, being given the opportunity to express their feelings can be very important to victims.

Getting Nothing Back

Many victims want the chance to talk directly to their offenders, even if they get nothing back. This was dramatically highlighted for me during the much-publicized trial of Olin Ferguson. Ferguson randomly shot and killed passengers traveling on a crowded Long Island Railroad commuter train. Despite the public nature of his crime, with innumerable witnesses, Ferguson proclaimed his innocence. Obviously insane, he nonetheless served as his own defense attorney at his trial. Each day of the trial I saw witnesses and survivors interviewed on television expressing their satisfaction at having had the chance to speak directly to the offender, unlike in normal proceedings where attorneys would have separated the offender from the victims. Clearly the victims were getting nothing back from Ferguson. He was living in another reality. Yet even without Ferguson expressing remorse or acknowledging his actions, the opportunity to address the killer was helpful to many of the people who had been terrorized by his mad rampage.

The victim must have the ultimate choice of whether or not to confront the offender. Some will not choose the opportunity. Others may prefer to wait. But under our present system of justice victims and those who care about them almost never get the chance to express themselves directly to the offender.

CHAPTER 9

Shame

Some people have confused conferencing with recently publicized efforts by some criminal court judges to shame offenders into changing their ways—a modern-day equivalent of the 17th century practice of making adulterers publicly wear a scarlet letter A on their clothing. The confusion arises from the use of the word "shame" in association with conferencing. The critical distinction is between stigmatizing shame and reintegrative shame. Reintegrative shame is a concept of the Australian criminologist John Braithwaite. His book *Crime, Shame and Reintegration* was published in 1989, coincidentally the same year that New Zealand initiated family group conferencing.

Reintegration

While Tomkins's affect theory, as articulated by Donald Nathanson, serves as the psychological explanation for the effectiveness of conferencing, Braithwaite provides the sociological explanation. Braithwaite observes that those societies that reintegrate rather than stigmatize offenders have the lowest crime rates. Even without the extremes of a scarlet-letter approach, our current justice and school disciplinary systems deal with offenders in a way that makes it difficult for them to shed their "offender" label. We punish, fine, reprimand, incarcerate, detain, suspend and expel but pay little or no attention to repairing the real harm done to the victim and the community. On the other hand, restorative justice strategies like conferencing allow offenders to make amends, repair the harm, apologize, gain acceptance and be reintegrated into the community.

Shame, Tomkins teaches us, is a fundamental affect and occurs spontaneously. A conference is not convened for the purpose of shaming someone; rather, shame arises automatically and naturally in offenders and their families when confronted with the reality of the offenders' wrongdoing. No matter how a society addresses wrongdoing, the act of doing so will inevitably foster shame. But Braithwaite advises that the experience should be *reintegrative, not stigmatizing.* He warns that failing to reintegrate offenders only encourages the development of negative subcultures.

We commonly see evidence of growing negative subcultures gathered on urban street corners or in schools. Youths who see themselves as "bad" align themselves with other youths who have negative self-images. Among the latter, being "bad" is a badge of honor. No longer identifying themselves with the mainstream, they reject mainstream values. Clearly something is wrong when so many feel like outcasts in their own communities. We need to reassess whether our current approach to wrongdoing is making things better or worse.

Braithwaite, as a criminologist, adopted a novel approach to the question of crime. Rather than asking "Why do criminals do the wrong thing?" he asked, "Why do most people do the right thing most of the time?" His conclusion is that most people do the right thing because they want to please the people they care about and avoid displeasing them. So the opinions of family and friends are a powerful source of social control, especially when we are young. As adults, most mature human beings have internalized this dynamic into the form of a "conscience." As adults we do the right thing because we believe in doing the right thing. But fear of being shamed, of displeasing those who love and care about us, still serves to reinforce our sense of right and wrong.

When we videotaped an interview with Braithwaite in Australia he talked about the Maori, the indigenous people of New Zealand, whose practices influenced the initial development of conferencing. "For them the Western way of transacting justice is barbaric," he said. "To have the offender stand alone, isolated, confronting the guilt of his offenses, is an act of barbarism. And their conception of shame, the Maori conception of shame, *whakama*, is the shame that you feel in the eyes of your community. It's not the Western idea of individual guilt. It's a communitarian kind of shame. And therefore, they say that what ought to happen is that the accused person ought to stand surrounded by those who love and care for him, those who are respected by him. They're the people who can shame effectively, and they're the people who can offer social support during a difficult time."

I have been repeatedly advised that this approach is typical of native or aboriginal peoples around the world. An African woman at a talk I gave in Philadelphia told me that the restorative conference resembles the process her father, a chief, would conduct to address a crime in his community. I mentioned earlier that the representatives of Cree and Ojibwa villages who came to our Real Justice trainings spoke about the similarity with their traditional practices, and I have heard Navajo and other Native Americans concur. Long before modern societies developed their stigmatizing practices, we allowed offenders to be reintegrated into their communities. Perhaps we need to return to what we left behind.

Tomkins said that shame is "one step removed from heaven" because shame can exist only when someone wants to re-establish a bond. Offenders must care about their relationships with others to feel shame. Our criminal justice and school disciplinary systems fail to capitalize on the opportunity to use that shame in a constructive way. They stigmatize and alienate offenders, driving them toward the other outcasts in our society who comprise the growing negative subcultures.

Compass of Shame

Donald Nathanson defined four general patterns or "scripts" to describe how people respond to their shame: *withdrawal, avoidance, attack self* and *attack other*. He organized them as the four directions on a "compass of shame" (see Figure 2). *Withdrawal* is marked by escape, by running from the shameful situation. *Avoidance* involves trying to ignore the shame, perhaps by using drugs and alcohol or distracting oneself with pleasurable indulgences. *Attack self* involves blaming or feeling disgusted with oneself. *Attack others* involves displacing the feeling of shame by blaming someone else.

The four scripts are normal reactions to shame, but in excess they are very destructive. We can see young wrongdoers accumulating burdens of shame, usually first in school and then in the community. They demonstrate all four patterns on the compass of shame, increasing as each new offense brings greater stigmatization and alienation from mainstream society. Drinking and drugging, joyriding in cars, running away from home, missing school, lying and making excuses, blaming others, attempting suicide, bullying and committing violence are some of the harmful vehicles young offenders choose to travel in all directions on the compass of shame. Conferencing, on the other hand, addresses wrongdoing in a way that allows young offenders to resolve their shame by making amends, repairing the harm they have caused and earning acceptance and often forgiveness. If, at the earliest grade levels in schools, children's inappropriate behavior were systematically challenged with a reintegrative response, such as restorative conferencing, many would never begin their climb up the ladder of stigmatization and alienation.

THE COMPASS OF SHAME
Figure 2

Withdrawal:
> isolating oneself
> running and hiding

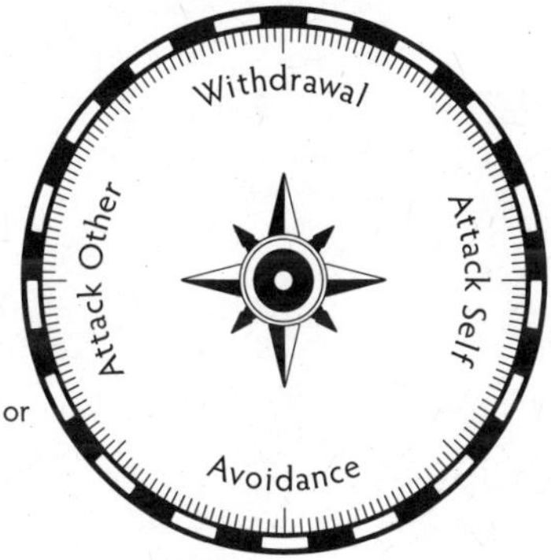

Attack Other:
> "turning the tables"
> blaming the victim
> lashing out verbally or
  physically

Attack Self:
> self put-down
> masochism

Avoidance:
> denial
> abusing drugs and alcohol
> distraction through thrill-seeking

ADAPTED FROM NATHANSON, 1992

CHAPTER **10**

On Our Own

We invited the Australians back to do trainings one more time in October 1995. We had 150 trainees in Pennsylvania and 200 in Minnesota, more participants than we anticipated, but in our enthusiasm for conferencing we felt reluctant to turn anyone away. To deal with the large number of trainees we asked individuals who had facilitated conferences since the first training to help as "coaches" when small groups of trainees role-played restorative conferences.

From the outset we recognized that we could not afford to keep flying Australians back and forth across the Pacific and would have to develop our own training capability. Our first efforts began before the Australians returned for their second visit. We converted the printed materials that had been distributed in loose-leaf format at the first training into a training manual that we had printed and bound as a book. We also produced a video that showed an actual restorative conference conducted by a police officer for two young female shoplifters. Both the manual and the video were helpful new educational resources for trainees.

As I parted ways with my Australian friends at the Minneapolis-St. Paul airport, I knew we were on our own, and I felt a heavy burden of responsibility. Not only did my staff and I have to gain more experience with conferencing ourselves and then learn to train others, but we had to develop an economically viable program to sustain our mission of spreading conferencing across North America.

Training and Educational Resources

Starting with a training for a group of elementary school educators in February 1996, we began a careful and systematic effort to refine the training program originally presented by the Australians. After each successive training we scrutinized the participant evaluations, compared our own perceptions with one another and then made changes.

Our long-term goal was to develop a facilitator training that could be licensed to government or nonprofit agencies throughout Canada and the United States, so that the training effort could be localized and the cost dramatically reduced. We saw our Real Justice program as developing the training, the educational resources, the training-of-trainers and the ongoing support system.

We developed a series of "mini" role plays for the training that would allow participants to practice facilitating conferences. Each successive role play grows more difficult as the training progresses because we spike each with more difficult challenges for the conference facilitator. In the first role play the characters' roles are cooperative but thereafter some individuals become abusive or get the group off track, problems that occasionally arise in real conferences. We produced a 17-minute introductory videotape, which we sell for a nominal fee as a resource for anyone who has to present the concept of restorative conferencing. We also developed four videos for the training program. Trainers are provided with a detailed, step-by-step outline, accompanied by a set of overhead projector transparencies. The outline spells out how to set up the room, defines the goals for each training segment, and cues trainers for each of the transparencies and videos. Our goal was to make the training outline, resources and training-of-trainers so comprehensive and of such high quality that trainers consistently offer a good experience.

Research and Evaluation

At about the same time that we began to develop our own training program, we also initiated our own research effort. The only evaluation of conferencing for juvenile offenses to date had been done in Wagga Wagga, New South Wales. Another substantial evaluation was underway in the Australian Capital Territory for both juvenile offenses and adult drunk driving. We wanted an evaluation of conferencing in the United States. We were fortunate when a police lieutenant in Bethlehem, Pennsylvania, approached us about training officers to conference juvenile cases and applying for research funding from the National Institute of Justice, a division of the U.S. Department of Justice.

I had just met Paul McCold, a college professor and researcher, who was passionate about restorative justice and enthusiastic about collaborating with me on a grant proposal. The Bethlehem police commissioner strengthened our research design by allowing us to randomly assign cases either to conferencing or to the courts. Much to our delight, our proposal was approved for funding.

Bethlehem sits on the boundary of two counties, so we had to get approval and cooperation from two juvenile probation departments, two juvenile court judges, two district attorneys and a number of district magistrates who handled the offenses that are not referred to juvenile court. We reached agreement on the range of offenses that could be conferenced, including shoplifting, simple assault, disorderly conduct, vandalism and other lesser juvenile offenses.

The research project got under way just as our first trainings commenced. We were now on our own without the Australians' assistance, and we seemed to be getting off to a good start.

CHAPTER **11**

Police

The first family group conferences in New Zealand were facilitated by social workers. Not until Terry O'Connell, the Australian cop, devised his own version of conferencing did police officers become involved as facilitators. There have been critics of police conferencing ever since.

When I was just starting Real Justice, a woman who was trying to initiate a victim-offender mediation program in a nearby county disparaged the idea of police facilitating conferences. "Don't police have better things to do?" she asked.

An academician warned me about "cop culture." He and others advised that police officers do not have the right temperament and mind-set to facilitate conferences. "They are attracted to policing by a need for power and authority," they said.

Others criticized the practice of police officers facilitating restorative conferences because police represent the power of the state and cannot be neutral. These critics insisted that conference facilitators, as in many victim-offender mediation programs, should be trained citizen volunteers so that neutrality can be assured. They expressed the fear that police will become both judge and jury.

Still others warned that police are not adequately sensitive to victims and their needs. In their effort to pull together the conference, police may pressure victims into a conference when they don't really want to participate.

I believe that these generalizations about police are unkind and unwarranted. While one might fairly describe the male-dominated profession of policing as more "macho" than most occupations, the police officers I know want to help people and want to make their communities safe. They are attracted to conferencing because they see its potential in helping victims get satisfaction and making offenders realize the harm they are doing in a way that the courts fail to do.

Problem-Oriented Policing

To say that police officers have "better things to do" contradicts the most progressive current thinking, such as Herman Goldstein's concept of "problem-oriented policing," which envisions police officers working as problem-solvers with the community, rather than only as law enforcers. Consider how the police officer's time is spent waiting outside courtrooms to testify in hearings that neither impact the offender nor serve the victim. Is it not better to use a police officer's time to conference a variety of offenses within days or weeks, rather than months, and achieve meaningful outcomes for victims, offenders and the community? How can anyone say that police have "better things to do"?

Those who suggest that citizen volunteers would be more neutral than police officers in running a conference confuse conferencing with mediation, where two parties of equal moral standing come together to resolve their differences and the third-party mediator avoids taking sides. Conferences involve situations where one person commits a crime or wrong against another and the two parties are not of equal moral standing. Given that the offender has admitted the offense, which is the prerequisite for holding a conference, then the victim has been wronged and the conference facilitator cannot, in all honesty, be neutral. The facilitator only needs to be fair. The person setting up the conference, whether a police officer or a civilian, must treat all the parties, including the offender, in a respectful manner. Those who worry about the police officer becoming both judge and jury simply do not understand conferencing. First, the offender has already admitted his or her guilt before coming to the conference. Second, the conference participants and not the facilitator are responsible for deciding the outcome. Only the victim and offender need agree. The process has no resemblance to a courtroom proceeding.

When police have inappropriately interfered in the conference, based on the experience of the researchers in the Bethlehem police conferencing project, it has happened during the agreement phase of the conference. Sometimes police facilitators recommended that the group consider community service for the offender when none of the participants suggested it. Although the facilitator is not supposed to intrude into the discussion with such a comment, citizen volunteers and other facilitators are as likely to do the same thing.

With respect to concerns about how police might treat victims, one of the fundamental lessons taught in the Real Justice facilitator training program is respecting the wishes of victims. There is no reason why police officers would be any less likely to hear that message than anyone else. The research supports that conclusion. At no time in the Bethlehem police conferencing project did researchers find evidence of police facilitators pressuring victims into attending the restorative conference.

Restorative justice advocates must include police officers, who comprise the largest group of criminal justice professionals, in their vision of the future. To fail to do so risks keeping restorative justice at the margins of the system. As Herman Goldstein learned from observing Chicago police in their daily routine, police officers have a wide range of discretion in the administration of justice. Their interactions with the community provide innumerable opportunities for a restorative, rather than punitive, approach to justice.

Real Justice can transform the role of police. Police officers are extremely open to conferencing once they see it work with their own eyes. "I've been a detective for 20 years and I was a bit cynical about it when I first heard about it," admitted an Australian police supervisor in an interview with me. He continued, "I thought it was a bit too airy fairy. And we looked at it and it was fully explained to us. And I was very keen to sit in on one of the conferences to see how it went before I made the decision. Having sat in on two in one night, I was quite surprised how well they went and how the people interacted and responded to it. And from there on it was full ahead with it."

I have seen cop after cop respond to conferencing first with professional skepticism, then with interest, finally with enthusiasm. A Bethlehem police officer came to our very first training and tried conferencing shortly thereafter. His enthusiasm was contagious. Soon his department's leadership decided to implement conferencing on a larger scale and collaborate on the research project. He said, "Conferencing is the most powerful experience I have had in my past 20 years of police work. It is very positive for victims in that they are able to have a say."

Similarly two Indianapolis police officers came with skepticism to a Pennsylvania training, but went home determined to try their own conferences. Without formal procedures in place to support conferencing, they had to find time to fit the conferences into their busy day. But their first efforts were extremely gratifying. Since then they have become Real Justice certified trainers and are part of a major effort to implement conferencing in the educational and criminal justice systems in Indianapolis and surrounding areas.

The RCMP (Royal Canadian Mounted Police) has taken a different approach to implementing conferencing. In those communities where they contract to provide local police service and in their involvement with aboriginal policing, the police develop a pool of community volunteers to run the conferences for the cases that they will refer to the volunteers.

In Sparwood, British Columbia, an RCMP sergeant and a defense attorney read an article about conferencing and decided to try it. The results have been remarkable. In most Canadian communities about 40 percent of juvenile offenders are rearrested. In Sparwood, where virtually all their juvenile cases in the last two years have been referred to conferencing and none to the courts, rearrest rates have plummeted to 8.3 percent in 1995 and to 2.9 percent in 1996.

Stolen Whale

Some police officers use conferencing more informally when it is not practical to convene a larger formal conference. My favorite example is the story of the stolen "whale." That's the way the report came over the radio—a report of a stolen whale. The police officer even checked it on his car's computer. He still read "whale." When he arrived at the indicated address and spoke with the victim, he realized that the man's southern accent had been misunderstood in the Midwestern town. Not a "whale" but an ornamental "well" had been stolen from his front yard. The officer soon apprehended Charlie, a teen-ager who admitted taking the well as a prank. While the officer wanted to handle the offense with a restorative conference, he learned that the victim was about to leave town for a couple of weeks on a vacation. So he held an impromptu conference then and there. Sitting in the victim's living room, Charlie talked about what he had done and then the officer asked the man to tell how the offense had affected him.

As is often the case with a so-called "minor" offense, the effect on the victim is far more substantial than the degree of economic loss. The real consequence is about a loss of safety, a sense that one's private space has been violated and a fear of further violations.

Given that the man was about to leave town, he was particularly fearful that other theft or damage might occur in his absence. To Charlie the theft of the well had been funny, but to the victim it was deeply disturbing. The theft also came at a hectic time when the man was rushing to make arrangements for his vacation. He still had many things to do, including finding someone to cut his lawn. Charlie offered to cut his lawn for him while he was away and an agreement was quickly reached.

Charlie sincerely apologized for what he had done, now aware that his action had been far more hurtful than he had ever imagined. The victim generously accepted the apology, much relieved that the incident had been resolved. Now he no longer worried about further theft or damage and he had someone to cut his lawn while he was gone.

The police officer had demonstrated a classic example of problem-oriented policing. The citizen later told all his friends and neighbors about the creative response to his problem, enhancing the community's view of the police. Charlie learned an important lesson and waved to the police officer whenever he saw him on patrol. And the police officer cruised by the house during the man's vacation and saw that the lawn was neatly mowed.

Runaway Couple

Other examples of problem-oriented policing include situations when the young person's behavior is not technically a crime, but some kind of response would be helpful. Two pairs of distressed parents reported that their respective son and daughter had run away together. The teen-age couple were found and returned to their home community a few days later. Ordinarily the police officer would have simply handed them over to their parents, explaining that there was nothing more he could do. But having learned to facilitate restorative conferences, the police officer realized that he could provide a meaningful service to the families and offered to run a conference. The parents and children agreed and the officer used the conferencing script to foster a meaningful dialogue for both families. Without attacking or accusing, but with tears flowing, each mother and father shared their feelings and fears with their children and recounted the hell they had experienced. The conference was far more effective than any punishment because the boy and girl saw the harm they had done to their parents. Rather than feeling resentment, they felt empathy.

True Confessions

It is remarkable how conferencing creates an atmosphere of genuine remorse and truthfulness, unlike the adversarial atmosphere of the courtroom where lawyers advise their clients to say as little as possible. A police officer was facilitating a conference for burglary of a retail store and suddenly, in the midst of the emotional exchanges between victims and teen-age offenders and parents, the offenders began to admit to other offenses. Lots of offenses. Not just their offenses, but those of friends. By the end of the conference dozens of burglaries had been explained, leading to a series of investigations and further conferences. Although there are legal limitations on the use of information obtained within the context of the restorative conference, the police officers in this case were able to use the information in a way that eventually resolved a great many thefts.

Police and other conference facilitators also have to be alert to revelations of abuse, which must be reported to the appropriate authorities, and to other issues that arise, like persistent conflict between parent and child that suggests the need for counseling. Police officers doing conferences may give parents and young people information about human services available in the community.

Some police have tried conferencing neighborhood disputes in which both sides have wronged one another. While police officers often intervene informally in such disputes, a properly prepared conference can provide a structured environment. Ideally the officer can get both parties ready to admit some responsibility for wrongdoing before the conference. The officer then uses the questions in the conference script to get both parties talking in terms of how they have been affected by the grievance, rather than simply accusing the other person. Parking spaces, barking dogs, noisy gatherings—these are issues that can lead to problems and violence unless people start to talk to each other in a real way and recognize each other's feelings.

Implementation

As police begin to use conferencing more systematically, different approaches to implementation are being tried. In Wagga Wagga, for example, there was a sergeants' committee that reviewed all of the juvenile cases for the week and decided which cases should be conferenced. The committee review had some indirect benefits in making officers more careful about their arrests. When the real offense was "contempt of cop," that is, when a youth was not adequately respectful of a police officer but committed no real crime, such an inappropriate arrest would be more readily detected when it passed through the hands of the sergeants' committee. According to Terry O'Connell such instances became less common.

Other police departments have assigned an individual officer to supervise cases, either by conferencing appropriate offenses himself or assigning them to other trained officers. Some departments limit conferencing to a few specialists while others have trained a large number of officers who conference cases in addition to their other responsibilities.

Police departments that do conferencing define a range of cases permissible for conferencing, usually having reached an understanding with officials of the court, such as the public prosecutor, public defender, juvenile court or president judge, or juvenile probation chief. In those communities where schools are doing conferencing, it is necessary to define which offenses may be handled within the schools themselves or by police officers who are assigned to the schools. Because conferencing is so new, most of the procedures and protocols are new and may evolve as time goes on.

Research Results

The Bethlehem police conferencing research project showed lower rearrest rates for offenders who chose conferences than for those who did not, making conferencing an excellent strategy for diverting youth from the criminal justice system. The study found that 96 percent of victims and 97 percent of offenders were satisfied with the conference process, with about half feeling "very satisfied," and 94 percent of the offenders completed the restitution and community service commitments they made in the conference. Significantly, the results of this first evaluation of conferencing in North America confirm the equally positive results of earlier research with police conferencing in Wagga Wagga, New South Wales, Australia, completed in 1995, and the preliminary results of a four-year study of police conferencing currently under way in the Australian Capital Territory with juvenile offenders and adult drunk drivers.

Also, the proportion of cases in the Bethlehem police conferencing study in which victims and offenders agreed to participate in conferences was higher than those agreeing to participate in victim-offender mediation (VOM), based on earlier studies of VOM, a restorative justice process that has been employed since the 1970s. These findings do not support the concern raised by some critics of police conferencing that victims and offenders are less trusting of police than of the trained volunteers and professionals who conduct VOM programs. The Bethlehem police conferencing study also found that conference participants reported a higher rate of satisfaction and sense of fairness than those who

answered identical research questions in those earlier VOM studies. The research clearly supports the contention that conferencing
by police is worthwhile. So, in answer to the critics, no, police do
not have better things to do.

CHAPTER 12

School

Schools are the breeding grounds for our society's negative subcultures. Schools do not intend to hurt children, but like much of the rest of our society they often respond to wrongdoing with punishment. They operate under the false expectation that punishment causes children to change their ways. The result of all those punitive writing assignments, detentions, suspensions and expulsions is a growing number of young people who see themselves as outcasts, as "bad." School disciplinary procedures, as in the criminal justice system, provide little or no opportunity for reintegration—for making amends, apologizing, repairing the harm or shedding the offender label. They exclude from the disciplinary process those most affected by the offense—the offenders, victims and their respective communities of care. The primary difference between schools and courts is that schools start alienating offenders at an earlier age.

Educators are no more to blame than anyone else. We all have grown up in a punitive system and have rarely questioned it. Like our politicians, school administrators keep trying to satisfy a concerned public by being tougher and punishing more severely. And we all have watched in dismay as outrageous behavior becomes more commonplace, despite police in the schools and an all-time high in the number of expulsions.

We must rethink our assumptions, not our goals. We must still demand appropriate behavior and accountability, but we can no longer rely on school administrators dictating outcomes. Rather, we should make offenders face the real consequences of their offenses by involving everyone who has been harmed. Family, fellow students and faculty members who have been affected need a forum to tell the offenders, in emotional terms, how they have been affected by that offender's inappropriate behavior.

The first restorative conference in a school setting took place in Australia at Maroochydore High School in Queensland in 1994. Since then conferencing has been used to respond to a wide variety of problems in elementary and secondary schools. ·

Pepper Mace

Two boys sprayed a whole can of pepper mace on classroom door handles in a high school hallway. The odor was so pervasive that hundreds of students were evacuated from the building, with some students and faculty experiencing serious allergic reactions to the caustic fumes. The police had been contacted, so when the two youths were discovered and admitted their offense, the normal administrative response would have been to press criminal charges and suspend or possibly expel the students. Instead, a school district social worker who had been advocating for Real Justice was invited to facilitate a restorative conference with parents, faculty who had to evacuate the building and school administrators, who all felt very much victimized by the youths' actions. The formal outcome of the conference included written apologies and community service work for both youths.

The informal outcome was of greater significance, as expressed by the assistant principal whom I interviewed many weeks after the event. As the school disciplinarian, he acknowledged that he had dealt with the boys before, one in particular. He felt that the boy never fully appreciated how he affected other people with his previous misconduct. He was extremely pleased with the conference and believed, not only that the boys were genuinely remorseful, but also that they really understood the harm they had done to a great many people. He reported that all of the administrators and faculty were pleased to have had an opportunity to vent their feelings. The conference had satisfactorily resolved the matter.

Phone Prank

In another high school incident, a girl suddenly found her face stuck to a pay phone's earpiece that had been coated with a fast-drying glue as a practical joke. The perpetrators, who thought the incident was incredibly funny, gained a whole new perspective from the restorative conference. They had to face their victim and hear her describe her terror when she first realized what happened. She described how pieces of her skin remained stuck to the phone when it was finally removed. Her emotion in retelling the story resonated in them. They felt her fear and pain and embarrassment. Had they been suspended from school, their resentment would have shielded them from their victim's feelings and a real understanding of what they had done to another human being.

False Rumor

In another school several boys deliberately spread a false rumor that a girl had been masturbating during class. By the next school day the story was all over the school. When one of her friends told her, she burst into tears, then sought out the guidance counselor for advice.

With the support of the school administration, the guidance counselor decided to conference the incident. She realized that having the boys punished would distract from the real issue, the humiliation they had caused this young woman. If the focus shifted to punishment, there would be debate on whether it was too strong for what some might regard as a mere youthful prank or too light.

The guidance counselor did not contact the parents directly, which she knew was contrary to normal conferencing procedure. Rather, she called the boys into her office and told them that she had heard about the rumor and wanted them to come in with their parents to the school the next day. As she subsequently related to me, she found herself wondering about the conversation at the dinner table when the boys tried to tell their parents why they had to come to school the next day.

The conference was very powerful. No one could even think of minimizing the impact on the girl after she tearfully related how she came to hear about the rumor and how terrible she felt. She wondered why they did this to her. One of the boys' fathers had tears in his eyes, and everyone in the room was deeply moved. When it came to deciding the consequence, the girl simply said, "I don't want you to do anything. I just want it to end." That was that. The boys and their parents apologized profusely and everyone left the room. They all went back to their daily activities, but not as if nothing had happened. Although no one was punished, the girl felt better because her feelings had been acknowledged by everyone at the conference. Without the boys promoting the rumor, it faded away.

Elementary School Incidents

In younger grades, conferencing is equally effective. One of the first elementary school conferences I heard about involved a serious assault by a third-grade boy against a fourth-grade boy on the playground. The conference, which was also attended by the boys' mothers, had a powerful impact on the offending boy and his subsequent behavior.

People ask how young an offender can be successfully conferenced. I suggest that as soon as children can talk and understand language, they can be meaningfully involved in a conference. I am aware of a kindergarten child being conferenced for trying to trip the secretary in the elementary school office. Although his mother was resistant to the event and after the conference referred to it as a "kangaroo court," the little boy was pleased. He told some of his classmates how glad he was that the conference helped him and that he was no longer in trouble. His mother later admitted that the conference had been a good experience for her son.

The little boy in question is exactly the kind of child who begins the downward spiral into negativity even as he begins his school experience. His negative behavior is punished and early on he gets a reputation as a "bad kid." Feeling like a bad kid and having no clear path to redeem his reputation as he moves through his school years, he eventually seeks the company of the other "bad kids" in his school who reinforce each other's negative behavior.

Children need limits and effective discipline. We do not serve children well if we are permissive and fail to confront inappropriate behavior. Confronting that behavior in a reintegrative way is far better than punishing and labeling children.

Role Plays as Prevention

We do not have to wait for children to do something wrong to help them gain empathy and insight into the harm caused by violence and other misconduct. Elementary teachers and guidance counselors are beginning to use role plays of conferences as a prevention technique. I observed a role play organized by an elementary guidance counselor in a sixth-grade classroom. The imaginary but commonplace incident involved a girl who had been consistently ridiculed by two boys in her class to the extent that her parents called the school when she said she didn't want to go to school anymore. Beforehand the guidance counselor had discussed the concept of role play with the students, described the role-play incident, asked for volunteers to assume roles, and then gave those who had roles some time to discuss how they thought the individuals would feel and what they might say.

The next day the role-play conference was convened. The conference participants formed a circle in the center of the room with the guidance counselor acting as facilitator. The rest of the sixth-grade class and invited guests, like myself, sat around the room to observe.

Except for the size of the people in the chairs and their youthful voices, the role play was remarkably realistic. Those playing parents said what parents would say, and those playing principal and teacher did the same. The girl playing the victim actually began to cry on cue. Except for one participant with a minor role who occasionally smiled self-consciously and glanced at a classmate in the audience, everyone played his or her role to the hilt. As often happens in role plays, the imaginary event began to feel real and the actors became their characters. I found myself feeling quite moved.

The class discussion after the role play ended was also remarkable. The students immediately identified the same key questions that a group of adults would address. Is punishment effective? Would this kind of emotional event be more likely to change hurtful behavior? Would this help the victim?

The guidance counselor told me after the conference that the boy who played the father of the victimized sixth-grade girl in the role play often plays the role of the bully and the tease in real life. She felt that having him take the role of a caring father whose daughter was victimized would help him gain some insight into the impact of his own hurtful behavior and empathy for his victims. I do not know whether it changed his behavior.

Truancy

Conferencing can also be used for school offenses that are victimless, such as truancy. Parents and others who have been affected by the young person's behavior are informally the victims in the conference.

Joan was sent to an alternative school by her probation officer when she returned home after completing a residential drug-and-alcohol treatment program. Her attendance was satisfactory for a short time, then she missed more and more school. Having exhausted all the usual strategies to encourage attendance, Joan's program counselor asked another counselor to organize a restorative conference, since he felt too frustrated with his counselee to facilitate the conference himself.

The facilitator invited Joan's mother and father, her probation officer and, of course, the counselor who initiated the conference. When she asked who should act as a support, Joan wanted to bring her friend Eva, with whom she probably used drugs on the days she missed school. The facilitator hesitated, wondering how Eva might influence the conference, but she decided to go along with Joan's request.

The conference was emotional. Joan's parents were in tears, and her father told her how frightened he was each time the program counselor called him at work to say that his daughter had not arrived at school. He would imagine finding her overdosed and dead. Everyone agreed that missing school was a clear indicator that she was using drugs again. Her probation officer said that he could not allow Joan to continue violating her probation and endangering herself. He was considering a long-term residential treatment placement.

Eva seemed to impact Joan most, perhaps because it was most unexpected. She cried and told Joan that she was her best friend and that she didn't want Joan to go away again. Eva pointed out what Joan needed to do to straighten out her life (although Eva probably should have been heeding her own advice).

In the agreement phase of the conference, Joan apologized to her parents, counselor and probation officer for all the problems and heartache she had caused. She agreed to attend Narcotics Anonymous meetings every day and to record an entry about each meeting in her journal. She also promised not to miss any more days of school. Even if she didn't feel well, she would at least report to school and find someone to give her a ride home if she still felt sick. All the adults were satisfied with the conference and were particularly pleased with the friend's contribution.

The participation of peers who are also getting in trouble can be appropriate in a conference. I have heard (but don't know details) of conferences where fellow gang members attended and made a positive contribution. The conference facilitator needs to make a judgment call whether to include potentially negative peers and should talk to the proposed support persons before allowing their participation.

In this case Joan followed through with her commitments. At first she would write only a sentence or two in her journal about the N.A. meetings she attended. Then she started to note what people said at the meetings in greater detail but never said anything about herself. Several weeks into her journal writing she began to proudly report that she had spoken at the meeting and record what she had said. Her attendance was impeccable. She finished the school year with flying colors.

Not all conferences go as well as Joan's. In a rather imperfect conference for a boy who was truant, the facilitator allowed the adults to dominate the agreement phase. She should have checked each proposed item in the agreement with the offender, asking him if he agreed before allowing any other suggestions. Instead she let the adults draw up the list and when it was completed, turned to the offender and asked him if he agreed. He got up without saying a word and left the building.

The conference facilitator realized that she had not run the conference properly. She apologized for her mistake but did not know what to do about it.

Surprisingly, the next day the boy came to school. And the next. And the next. Something in the conference had affected him, and he attended school regularly.

In still another seemingly imperfect truancy conference a friend of mine ran, he couldn't get anyone to say more than a few words. Jose lived with his grandmother, who came to the conference, and when the facilitator asked the grandmother how she had been affected by her grandson's truancy, she looked at her grandson sternly and said, "He knows how I feel." A fellow student and Jose's school counselor had only a little to say, appearing constrained by the tone the grandmother had set. The agreement was simply that Jose would attend school. The whole conference lasted about 20 minutes.

The facilitator blamed himself for what he felt was a disastrous event. He speculated whether he should have spent a lot more time with the grandmother beforehand so she would have been more comfortable. His concerns were unwarranted. Jose began attending school every day. Despite the brevity of the conference and the apparent lack of free expression of emotion, that one look and few words from his grandmother evidently spoke volumes to Jose.

Certainly there have been many truancy conferences that did not produce such sterling results. Conferences are not a panacea, but they can have a significant impact on a great many kids.

In Minnesota truancy is defined as seven unexcused absences. At that point it becomes a legal matter and is referred to juvenile probation. In Rice County, Minnesota, about 40 miles south of Minneapolis-St. Paul, the local junior high school intervened with a restorative conference, facilitated by the police officer assigned to that building, after the third unexcused absence. With an enrollment of about a thousand students, the junior high had between 30 and 40 truants each year for a five-year period. The year they introduced systematic use of conferencing the number of truants fell to five.

School conferencing is of special value to parochial and other private schools whose reputations are critical to attracting tuition-paying students. Part of the incentive for parents to send their children to private institutions is that they are supposed to be safer, sheltered from the drugs, violence and other issues that plague many public schools. When incidents do arise, private school administrators may often find themselves conflicted about what to do. React harshly and purge the menace? Sweep it under the carpet? Risk publicity and a loss of students? Risk antagonizing parents and alumni? Conferencing addresses the offense squarely, and parents and others are almost always satisfied with the outcome.

Conferencing is a promising response to behavior problems in schools, but it will require a change of mind-set and philosophy among some school administrators. A friend of mine was telling an assistant principal at a junior high school about conferencing. The administrator reacted with dismay. He said that all he had to do was look in his school district's disciplinary handbook to see what punishment was prescribed for the student's offense and then see that it was carried out. Why would he want to get involved with this conferencing stuff?

Some administrators are not only unwilling to be inconvenienced by such a process, but they are also not going to let anyone else do it. In one instance, a school administrator interfered in an appropriately authorized conference by expelling several of the students who had committed the offense before the conference was held but allowed others to participate in the conference. This cast a dark shadow on the subsequent conference and created a legal hassle about the uneven treatment of the offenders. Despite evidence that harsh punishment neither serves students nor improves behavior in schools, there are those who are simply stuck in ineffective ways. They would rather go down with the old ship than consider traveling on a new vessel.

CHAPTER 13

Campus

Conferences have been held on college and university campuses. Because most college students are adults under the law, parental involvement would occur only if the offender requested it. Nonetheless, "campus conferencing" is the same process—except an offending student might have roommates or other friends there for support if he or she did not want to include parents or other relatives.

Institutions of higher learning face the same issues as the rest of society: more inappropriate behavior, more crime, more violence and a notable lack of success in dealing with it. For colleges and universities, conferencing offers a meaningful way to address offenses with less risk of losing tuition-paying students or offending alumni. The college administrator or resident assistant could deal with a wide range of problems by involving those who have been affected and letting them decide the outcome.

Drug Overdose

Lon, a young man at a small college, overdosed on drugs and had to be rushed to the local hospital where he recovered. Lon and his brother both attended the school, and neither had previous disciplinary violations. The college administration did not want to ignore this serious incident so they convened a restorative conference.

Lon readily admitted the stupidity of what he had done. He said that taking drugs was not typical behavior for him.

Two key "victims" in this offense were the campus security officer and the school nurse, both of whom were responsible for responding to the emergency. The officer told the youth how disturbed he had felt to find someone in such a life-threatening situation, and the school nurse shared how frightened she had been that Lon might die. Lon was very moved by their sincere concern for his well-being and recognized that he had put them through an ordeal. He agreed to avoid such behavior in the future and, as part of the outcome, committed himself to a defined amount of community service work.

At the close of the conference Lon thanked everyone, including the conference facilitator, for addressing the incident with a conference. He said that by having a chance to talk with everyone, he felt less embarrassed. He had feared that he would spend the next couple of years on campus seeing people who had been involved and feeling that they would look at him as a "druggie" because of what he had done. Although he had been very nervous about the conference, he felt much better now that he had attended.

Team Conference

Another area of campus life where wrongdoing needs to be addressed more effectively is in sports. Inappropriate behavior is sometimes ignored because punishment has consequences for the whole team. Conferencing is an alternate response that heals rather than disrupts.

A friend of mine ran a conference for a college sports team torn by internal strife. Don, an excessively competitive student, had repeatedly antagonized his teammates. After Rick, the team captain, overheard him complaining about his teammates to a professor, the entire team stopped talking to Don.

Dissension poisoned the team's morale. The coach unsuccessfully tried to resolve the conflict, but after weeks of frustration he turned the issues over to a conference facilitator.

Don reluctantly agreed to the conference. The facilitator encouraged him to take responsibility for his behavior. As the conference began, Don apologized to his teammates for his negative behavior. He explained that his parents were getting divorced, his girlfriend had dropped him and his best friend just died. He accepted responsibility. With deep emotion, he asked his teammates to forgive him for his rude and inappropriate behavior.

Each team member had an opportunity to tell Don how his behavior had affected them personally and how he had disrupted team unity. Rick, however, refused to give up his anger and accept Don's apology. The rest of the team confronted Rick's stubbornness. A freshman expressed how disappointed he was in the captain's reaction, how he and the younger team members looked up to Rick as a role model.

Negative feelings resonated for some time with the conference providing a safe environment for the exchange of emotion. Gradually the focus shifted toward how to repair the harm. The team defined a plan for resolution of the issues and everyone, including Don and Rick, agreed to work together. By the end of the conference a feeling of cooperation and camaraderie had been restored. The coach, who invited my friend to facilitate the conference, was thrilled with the outcome and has since become an advocate of conferencing.

Campus crime, misconduct and other inappropriate behavior, as in the rest of society, is generally handled with little regard for the emotions of all involved. By defining the appropriate offenses for conferences with the local police and public prosecutor and institutional authorities and then systematically using conferencing, many perplexing and destructive incidents could be handled constructively, satisfying victims, offenders and everyone who cares about them.

CHAPTER 14

Court

The first conference I ever attended was for the arson incident described in Chapter 6, conducted under the auspices of a juvenile court. The two youths who had committed the offense had already been adjudicated and were in a detention center, awaiting placement in a long-term residential treatment facility. The conference was not diversionary, that is, it was not an alternative to juvenile court or school disciplinary procedures. Rather, it was a supplement to the existing court process and was intended to provide healing and closure for the victims, the offenders, their friends and families and the community.

Diverting an Assault

Courts can still divert cases after police referral. Usually a probation officer has discretion at the point of intake into the juvenile probation system or even afterward, when a probation officer is assigned the case. For example, a probation officer who had been assigned a male youth charged with assault decided to handle the case as a restorative conference. As the facilitator began contacting everyone in preparation for the conference, he realized that the probation officer had made a wise decision in diverting the case from court.

The offender, Alex, hit a smaller boy, David, at his high school. When the facilitator called Alex, the youth sounded confused and defensive. He was confused because months had passed since charges had been filed. Having no experience with police or courts, he assumed that the matter had been dropped. He was defensive because he blamed David for the incident. He explained that David had harassed him all afternoon, emptying a pencil sharpener full of shavings over his head near the end of class period. As they left the classroom, David continued to pursue him down the hall. Alex lost his temper and hit the smaller boy, who fell and hurt his head.

Alex, who was a good student and athlete, had been shocked to find himself suspended from high school for several days and charged with assault. He said that he was willing to participate in the conference, especially since it was his only alternative to going to juvenile court, but he still seemed to blame David for the incident. When the facilitator called David's home his mother was irate. She felt that Alex should be punished by the courts and was not happy about the restorative conference. When the facilitator explained the advantages of the conference—that she would a get a chance to say how she felt directly to Alex—she eventually agreed, if her son would want to participate.

In his phone conversation with David, the facilitator learned that Alex had been accurate in describing the events that preceded the assault. Admitting his harassing behavior, David insisted that Alex should not have hit him and was willing to participate in the conference.

The facilitator decided to visit Alex and his parents at their home. He knew that David's mother's moral indignation and anger would skyrocket if Alex tried to blame her son. He spent almost an hour encouraging Alex to take responsibility for the assault, even if he felt he had been provoked by David. At some point Alex began to realize that he had responded to the other youth's annoying behavior by hitting him, even though he had had other choices. So the responsibility for the assault was his, not David's. At the conference David's mother was still irate, even though the offender admitted his responsibility at the outset. She said that her family would never have pressed charges if Alex had at least apologized. Alex claimed that he had apologized, the very next day. The victim's mother looked at her son who hung his head and said, "I forgot to tell you." From that point on the conference went rather smoothly toward resolution, bringing to a satisfactory conclusion an incident that did not belong in the criminal justice system.

Coma Conference

The next conference was unusual. It was held in the home of a victim, who was in a coma, and it did not follow the conference script. Even though this was not a normal conference, the outcome was so positive that I feel compelled to include it in this book.

Ken and Tony had been drinking and doing drugs. Ken, who was driving that night, lost control and wrecked the car. Tony, in the passenger seat, was almost killed and remained in a coma. Tony's mother Rita devoted herself to caring for her son at home. Two years after the tragedy the probation officer in the case arranged for a restorative conference at Tony's home. Rita wanted the conference at home so Ken could see her son. Ken had not visited Tony since the car crash.

The conference began with a startling occurrence. When Ken entered the house, accompanied by the probation officer and the conference facilitator, he went to Tony's bedside. Tony abruptly sat up with a loud gasp and then fell back onto his bed, remaining in a coma. Rita explained that the doctor had warned her that, even in a coma, sometimes an individual may react strongly to the sound of a familiar voice.

The conference was held near the bed of the unconscious victim. The facilitator immediately abandoned the script, recognizing that Rita and Ken had known each other for years and that their discussion needed little facilitation. Rita began the conference by telling Ken she didn't know whether to tear his head off or hug him. She acknowledged that if Tony had been driving, Ken might easily have been the person in the coma. But she couldn't understand why Ken hadn't come to visit. Ken apologized and explained that he'd been afraid to visit, fearful that Rita wouldn't want to see him because of what he had done to Tony.

As the intensity of the exchange subsided, the facilitator raised the issue of the conference agreement. Rita wanted Ken to commit himself to a long-term drug-and-alcohol treatment program and make a promise to visit regularly. Ken readily agreed. As a result of the conference, a tremendous emotional burden for two unhappy individuals was cast off and replaced by a mutually supportive relationship.

Several months after the conference Rita said that her only regret about the conference was that it did not occur sooner. Ken successfully completed substance-abuse treatment, and Ken's and Rita's families had Easter dinner together.

Sex Offender

A conference can help reintegrate an offender into his family and his community. A probation officer facilitated a conference for Jerry, an adolescent offender who had spent two years in a sexual-offender treatment program after repeatedly fondling and, on one occasion, having sexual intercourse with his sister's little girl while serving as her babysitter. Other adult siblings of Jerry and his sister, none of whom lived locally, had criticized Jerry's sister for involving the police, perhaps not knowing the details of the offense and equating the sexual abuse with children "playing doctor."

Jerry's sister and her husband were at the conference but did not want their daughter present. Instead they read a letter their daughter had written to her Uncle Jerry. The offender took responsibility for what he had done and achieved some degree of reconciliation with his sister and brother-in-law. Most significantly Jerry agreed to contact their brothers and sisters and advise them that what he had done was very serious and warranted involving the police. That outcome was of great value to his sister, who had been inappropriately criticized by her own family.

Check Forger

I have heard some probation officers protest that they should not run conferences for their own clients. There are some advantages to doing so. A probation officer facilitated a conference for Ron, who, while on probation, forged some of his mother's checks.

Ron started the conference by apologizing. His mother was irate but often interrupted her anger with a joke. A frown appeared on Ron's face whenever she did this.

The stepfather talked about his disappointment. He said that he had a good relationship with Ron but now felt betrayed and didn't know how his trust would be restored.

As the conference proceeded the mother and her son bickered until, in an outburst of rage, Ron shouted at his mother to stop joking around, telling her he hated how she made everything into a joke.

A little later in the conference one of the girls who came to support Ron talked about how he and his mother reminded her of her relationship with her mother. She said that she and her mother loved each other but always fought until they went to family counseling. Now they got along a lot better. She wondered if Ron and his mother would be willing to go to counseling.

Both Ron and his mother said that they would be willing, but the mother was concerned about the cost. Because the probation officer was facilitating the conference, he was there to assure them that the court would be willing to pay for counseling sessions if both of them agreed to attend regularly. So the counseling was built into the conference agreement.

The conference had a positive effect on Ron. He kept his commitments, attended the counseling sessions faithfully and improved his relationship with his mother and stepfather. He even improved his school attendance and grades, although those issues were not addressed in the agreement.

Intolerant Probation Officer

Even when probation officers delegate the conferencing responsibility to others, probation officers still must be trained in conferencing and understand the conference dynamics so that they can appropriately support the process. Otherwise they can cause problems, as happened in a shoplifting conference facilitated by a counselor for the local juvenile probation department.

Barbara, the woman who owned the store, was enraged. Her store had suffered a lot of merchandise loss over the previous year. She believed that the offender, a young girl, had stolen from her many times. She welcomed the opportunity to vent her feelings at the offender.

But once the conference was convened, Barbara realized that the youth had not lived in the community long enough to be part of her long-term problem. Also the youth was extremely apologetic and willing to take responsibility for what she had done.

As is often the case, a victim who displays strong emotions can swing from intense negative feelings to intense positive feelings. In the agreement phase of the conference Barbara was remarkably generous and compassionate to the offender, who had suffered personal problems.

After the conference Barbara told the conference facilitator that if she could ever help the offender, she would. The probation officer who had seen Barbara's preconference anger was annoyed by her extreme emotional turnabout and showed her disapproving look on her face. Barbara recognized the disapproval and burst into tearful shame and anger. She was revictimized by the probation officer's ignorant intolerance. Whether or not probation officers facilitate the conference, they should be trained to understand that such swings of emotion are commonplace among victims in conferences.

In some communities conferencing has been initiated as a collaboration with other local agencies. In Bucks County, Pennsylvania, for example, juvenile probation officers may refer cases, before or after adjudication, to be conferenced by a pool of volunteers who are recruited and trained under the auspices of the local victim services agency. In Minneapolis, several community organizations are collaborating with the local courts and police by recruiting and training qualified volunteers to conference neighborhood crimes such as prostitution, drug-dealing and other street crimes that foster the deterioration of neighborhoods. Conferencing not only has the potential to change the way the courts deal with crime, but also to involve the public in a meaningful role as well.

CHAPTER 15

Corrections

The least developed but potentially one of the most valuable uses of conferencing is in corrections. Prisons and the parole system are ripe for innovation because, as currently constituted, they do not work. The notion of rehabilitation in our correctional institutions is largely a myth.

Prison life is about survival. Few prisoners reflect on their wrongs and feel remorse for what they have done to their victims. The environment of prison is so harsh that prisoners largely see *themselves* as victims and spend little time thinking about the true victims of their crimes.

Conference Role Play in Prison

When Terry O'Connell was visiting the United States, we convened a role play of a restorative conference in Graterford Prison, a large maximum security facility in Pennsylvania, with the cooperation of two inmates serving life terms—Ali Thurman Bonner (to whose memory I have dedicated this book) and Simon Khaadim Ahad Evans. These two inmates founded the "School of Hard Knocks," which provided a life-skills program to prepare young inmates to successfully stay out of prison, and another program for troubled youths who visited the prison. They were excited by conferencing and believed that it had important implications for preventing crime and violence among youths. The role play dealt with Jay, who was serving a five-year sentence for shooting another youth in a dispute over the right to sell drugs on a street corner in Philadelphia. We asked a police officer who had recently been trained in conferencing to facilitate the conference. Terry, my wife Susan and several inmates volunteered to play the victim, the victim's relatives and Jay's relatives. Lacking women for all the female roles, I played the offender's mother. Jay participated in the conference as himself.

The role play may sound comical, but it was not. The conference was imaginary, but the shooting had been very real. Within minutes everyone was quite serious and immersed in their roles. We had no difficulty imagining the anger and disgust we would feel if someone hurt a member of our family, nor our shame if our son or brother were arrested for harming someone else. The role play was a powerful emotional experience for all of us.

Even though Jay had served three years of his sentence, he had never thought about all the implications of his crime. Ali later reported that Jay spent a couple of tearful hours on the telephone, apologizing to his mother for the harm he had done to his family.

In a video interview Jay said, "With the family conference, I realized that I hurt so many people. I didn't just hurt the victim. I hurt my family members, people around me, everybody that's got to deal with me and I got to deal with them. I hurt everybody. I hurt a lot of people."

Although I have some difficulty imagining spending three years in prison without realizing the harm I had done to my family, I am not Jay and have not had to walk in his shoes. Clearly restorative conferencing touched him and made him more empathetic than he had been before. Imagine what the real conference might have accomplished.

We have secured the cooperation of interested state and local corrections officials who want to experiment with conferencing for both juvenile and adult offenders. In addition to the possibility of inmates experiencing conferences with actual victims or in conference role plays, we also envision using conferencing as a response to probation and parole violations. Rather than automatically returning an offender to a prison or juvenile detention center, depending on the violation, conferences may allow the offender to face the violation squarely, experience the emotional consequences, make amends and take steps to remedy any harm that resulted. Too often an offender is returned to confinement when a meaningful interim step may be more appropriate.

Disciplinary incidents in prisons and detention centers also present opportunities for worthwhile conferences. Disciplining inmates for breaking rules or for offenses against other inmates or staff does not resolve the feelings that caused or resulted from the incident. A conference gets at the roots of the conflict and reduces the chance for a recurrence.

Each incident that is conferenced presents another opportunity for inmates to see the real consequences of their impulsive behavior. Punishment, on the other hand, gives inmates another opportunity to see themselves as victims and make excuses for what they have done. Many inmates go through their entire lives without ever really looking at themselves, because their homes, schools and communities have always responded with stigmatizing punishment that allowed them to be passive and resent authority. Conferencing holds offenders accountable in that they have to talk and think and experience other people's feelings.

Unlike with school, police and court conferencing, there has been little experience with corrections conferencing. Given the impact of conferencing with offenders in other settings, however, there is good reason to expect that conferences in correctional institutions and the probation and parole system will prove worthwhile.

Even if re-offense rates do not decline, the value to victims who want to face offenders is reason enough. We have to keep reminding ourselves that conferencing is, first and foremost, a service that we can offer to victims.

Returning from the Institution

The teen-age victim, Colin, had been involved in a fight with four other youths when the police intervened. Although the youth seemed to have no serious injuries, that night he experienced convulsions and fell into a coma. The four offenders were arrested and the juvenile court judge sent them all to residential treatment facilities for at least six months, after which their cases would be reviewed. In the meantime Colin emerged from the coma, but had suffered physical impairment to his motor functions and speech.

During the six months the four offenders were away the probation officer visited Colin and his family. The youth had experienced some physical improvement through intensive rehabilitation, but he and his family were filled with anger. Colin openly talked about revenge, promising to find each of the offenders when they returned to the community and get back at them, one at a time. The probation officer, recognizing that this family desperately needed a way to get some resolution and move beyond their anger, suggested the possibility of a restorative conference. Although Colin dismissed the idea at the time, the probation officer felt that he had given the victim and his family something to think about.

When the six months had elapsed, the four youths were escorted back to the juvenile court by counselors from the residential institutions. Colin and his family also attended the review hearing. The judge decided that the four offenders would be reassigned from secure treatment to foster homes closer to their home communities.

The probation officer decided to use the opportunity provided by the court hearing, which had brought everyone together, to again offer a restorative conference. Having had several months to think about the conference idea, Colin and his parents now expressed interest in participating. The offenders agreed as well. Although the offenders' parents were not at the hearing, the probation officer asked the residential counselors to serve as their supports in the conference.

In a small room, the only one available, the probation officer assembled the conference. Following the script, the conference provided an opportunity for everyone to talk, unlike the review hearing that just proceeded it. Colin had played no role in the review hearing. Also, he had been in the hospital when the offenders went through their initial court hearing. This was the first time that the offenders had seen Colin since the assault.

As Colin walked and spoke and gestured, his impaired functions were starkly demonstrated. The four offenders began to realize the damage they had done to another human being. One of them began to cry. Feelings are contagious, and soon all four offenders offered tearful apologies to the injured boy and his parents. Colin and his parents, moved by the sincerity of the four youths, readily offered their forgiveness.

The probation officer watched in amazement as the conference process worked its magic. The four offenders, long detached from the reality of their crime, faced what they had done and repented. Colin, until now obsessed with thoughts of revenge, and his parents freed themselves from anger and put closure on a horrible episode in their lives.

Rape and Murder

Ironically, the most compelling examples of the good that can result from face-to-face encounters between victims and offenders have been carried out with the most heinous crimes. I recently spent four gut-wrenching days at a training in which I heard from a panel of families of murder victims, visited a prison to hear from a panel of men convicted of murder, and watched hours of videotape of meetings between families of murder victims and murderers.

While we may recoil from the idea of ever facing the monsters who could do such horrible things to us or to people we love, after seeing the videotapes I have no doubt that for many victims and their families, the benefits are critical. For those who choose to proceed, the opportunity to express feelings directly to the offender and to ask questions can provide healing. One father of a murdered child, who was at our training all four days, assured us that meeting his daughter's killers was a critical step in putting some closure on the worst experience of his life.

Another father told us how the man who raped and murdered his child, after being convicted, turned toward the victim's family on his way out of the courtroom and gestured at them with his middle finger. Obviously that father and his family have absolutely no interest in meeting with such a lunatic.

But where the offender is willing to meet, to answer questions, to express remorse, even if he does not take full responsibility for his actions, families can begin to reconstruct the story of their lives. People who experience violent crimes have had the fabric of their life torn apart. They need to get answers to mend their understanding. Why me? Or why my loved one? They need to know details. How did she die? Did she suffer? What did she say? What did you say? What did you do? They want the truth.

Many of their questions can be answered only by the offender, and the process may take many hours. Strangely, they and the offender have the offense as a common bond. Talking and questioning and expressing feelings seems to bring the victim or the victim's family to a point where they can finally begin weaving new sections in their life story, whereas before the meeting they were endlessly stuck in trying to patch holes that could never be mended.

The offenders also gain from the encounter. Many of them committed violent crimes in fits of anger or while using alcohol or drugs, which allowed them to do things that they might never have done when they were sober. The offenders who agree to participate seem to do so out of a genuine interest in helping the victims or the victims' surviving family and friends. But sometimes they gain forgiveness as well.

I left the training emotionally drained but in absolute awe of the resilience of the human spirit. And I realized that isolating offenders and victims as we do, making such encounters the exception rather than the rule, is a terrible mistake.

To date, victim-offender mediators have been the pioneers in bringing serious offenders together with their victims or victims' families. But I trust that conferences will soon occur, probably involving more family members and close friends of the victims and offenders than the victim-offender mediations. Conferences involving severe offenses will require substantial preparation and will not occur until at least several years after the crime.

Most offenders will emerge from prison into our society with less understanding and compassion than when they entered. Most victims will struggle with their anger and their fear much longer than necessary, and in some cases indefinitely. Not everyone will choose to participate in conferences for serious offenses, but for those who are interested and willing, we ought to offer them an opportunity for real justice.

CHAPTER **16**

Workplace

Samantha, just out of college, had a noisy party at her apartment. Without her knowledge, a young man who was one year younger than the legal drinking age was among the many guests. When a police officer stopped to tell the group to quiet down, he also randomly checked the identification of some of the guests and discovered the young man drinking alcoholic beverages. Besides charging the underage guest, he also charged the hostess with "corrupting the morals of a minor." When Samantha expressed fear that such a charge threatened her job as a counselor at a program for delinquent youths, the police officer assured her that the charge was routine and that the public prosecutor would treat the matter lightly.

The police officer was wrong. When Samantha went to the initial hearing without an attorney, she realized that the matter was being taken very seriously. Although the criminal charge jeopardized her position as a youth counselor, she said nothing to her work supervisors during the months the wheels of justice slowly turned, although she had many opportunities. Everyone at work found out about her troubles when her name and the offense appeared in the newspaper.

The program director phoned Samantha to explain that "corrupting the morals of a minor," unless extenuating circumstances were thoroughly justified and documented, were usually grounds for automatic dismissal from her job. Further, she had undermined her supervisors' trust by keeping the offense secret for months. He asked if she would be willing to handle the situation with a workplace conference and explained what that meant. He said that he did not have the same emotional reaction to the situation as her direct supervisors and felt he could appropriately facilitate the conference. She agreed to the conference, not entirely sure what the alternative would have been.

At the conference the next day Samantha apologized profusely. Both supervisors told her bluntly how foolish she had been. Not only could they have guided her to a good attorney, but also they and her coworkers could have provided emotional support. They both felt they had a friendly and mutually respectful relationship with her and were shocked and hurt that she had kept the truth from them, particularly for such a long time. Her coworker whom she had nominated as her support agreed that it was tough, but he also admitted feeling badly that she had not trusted him enough to share her problems.

Samantha was reduced to tears. She said that she always had a hard time bringing up embarrassing problems and that she realized now she had hurt people who had trusted her.

Samantha profusely apologized to her supervisors. The agreement produced by the conference stated that she would work with her supervisors to address the criminal charge. The program director had arranged for refreshments after the conference and the young woman, her coworker and her supervisors all had an opportunity to talk informally before returning to work. Eventually the charge was dropped, and Samantha kept her job.

Instead of convening a conference, the program director could have called the counselor to his office for a verbal reprimand, given her a written reprimand that would also be copied to her personnel file, put her on probationary status or simply fired her. But the conference allowed everyone affected by her poor judgment and lack of trust to deal with their feelings, so she could make amends, shed her offender label and begin to repair the harm she had done to her relationships with her supervisors and coworkers.

Wrongdoing and inappropriate behavior in the workplace are usually handled badly. Aside from how the offense or behavior itself is addressed, workplaces rarely respond to the emotional implications of the problem. Morale and productivity are casualties of the unresolved feelings of the offending employee, their coworkers and supervisors. A workplace conference, which provides a forum for everyone who has been affected to express feelings and help shape the outcome, is a far less disruptive approach to addressing employee problems. An employee who has been confronted in a conference is less likely to feel resentful and victimized by the supervisor and more likely to see how he affected others and change his behavior.

Supervision and Evaluation

Sometimes the conferencing process identifies employees who are not willing to accept constructive supervision. Lana, an employee whose inappropriate behavior had raised serious concerns with her supervisors, was offered an opportunity for a workplace conference. Although the conference process was explained in the most supportive terms, the woman decided to quit her job instead. For both the company and the supervisors, Lana's decision to leave was a benefit of the conferencing process.

Conferencing can also be a useful evaluation. Aspects of personality and values may emerge in a conference that cause you to see that person differently, as the following story illustrates.

Louise, a bank loan officer, helped an unemployed friend get a small business loan by knowingly allowing her friend to list her previous job as current employment. Later, the misrepresentation came to light, but Louise was a valued employee, and bank management decided to handle her offense with a workplace conference.

At the conference, although Louise admitted what she had done, she tried to distinguish her offense from taking money from the bank for herself. Even though her supervisors and colleagues acknowledged that it was not as serious as stealing, Louise failed to appreciate that her offense was significant and to show evidence of regret. She kept saying her friend had repaid the loan and that she herself had derived no financial gain from the transaction.

The loan officer was not fired. She was demoted to less independent status in making loans. Significantly, she was no longer perceived as a candidate for promotion to management. Had she responded appropriately her offense would have been viewed as a lapse in an otherwise commendable career. Through the conference, however, she had demonstrated a character flaw that precluded further advancement at that bank.

Complex Dispute

Sometimes workplace conferencing is confused with mediation or other conflict resolution strategies, but conferencing is a deliberately emotional strategy. The script, with its open-ended questions, repeatedly asks participants how they were affected. Although we perceive ourselves as creatures of reason, our feelings are the key to resolution of conflict.

Harry had always been in conflict with his coworkers. He wanted to return to his job in a heavy industrial plant after a long disability leave, but found the company unwilling to have him back. The union supported Harry, but his immediate coworkers, who were also union members, supported the company's position. The complex dispute had dragged on more than a year when the company and the union agreed to allow a workplace conference facilitator to try to break the impasse.

Without a singular incident or clear admission of wrongdoing, the case was not one that would typically be handled as a workplace conference, but the conference facilitator was satisfied that Harry was willing to admit that he could be nasty and argumentative. He convened the conference on that basis.

The conference was tumultuous. The workers, union and company representatives did not respectfully wait for each person to finish speaking. They interrupted and shouted. The facilitator kept the conference within boundaries, but they were broader boundaries than usual.

Harry admitted that he could be an "S.O.B." Some of the coworkers reminded him of fights he had provoked. Other coworkers were willing to admit acts of revenge, like nailing Harry's boots to the floor of the locker room. But after an hour of loud argument the issue of what to do about Harry was still not resolved.

Among Harry's supporters at the conference was his sister. When the facilitator asked how she was affected by Harry's negative behavior, she acknowledged Harry could be a difficult person. But then she proceeded to tell the entire group the story of their childhood, of their violent, drunken father and his rampages, of Harry's courage in protecting his siblings, of the night her father broke a chair over Harry's back when he defended the family against his violence. There wasn't a dry eye at the conference. A whole new perception of Harry emerged and a new understanding of why he was such a difficult person.

Harry himself was so choked with emotion that the facilitator adjourned the conference. He and his sister went out for a breath of air. By the time they returned, the company and the union had reached an agreement. Although Harry would not return to work, the company made a cash settlement in the form of a trust fund that would pay him a regular stipend in addition to his existing pension benefits.

Everyone agreed that this was an equitable way to resolve the dispute. After more than a year of wrangling between company and union representatives and their respective attorneys, the free flow of human emotion washed away the two parties' differences and a settlement was achieved.

Human beings are creatures of emotion.

Family Business

In another conference, two principals in a family business came together to confront differences that had simmered for a long time. Each party had unresolved feelings toward the other that had affected the company. Employees had taken sides with one owner over the other. Snide comments were being muttered under people's breath. Mocking looks were exchanged when backs were turned. In short, the company was becoming an unhealthy and conflict-ridden place to work. A third owner, also a member of the family, convinced the two feuding owners to participate in a work-place conference.

The facilitator tried to get each party to take some responsibility for his own behavior, but neither was ready to make a clear-cut admission. So she brought them together and asked each of them questions about how the other person's actions had affected them. On one occasion the conference broke down when one of the owners stormed out of the room. At that point, in private conversation, the facilitator cautioned the individual who left that unless he and his co-owner settled their issues and reversed the negative environment they had created in their company, there wasn't going to be a company in a couple of years. The owner returned to the conference.

The intense exchange of emotion that occurred in the safety of the conference allowed issues to be aired. Many issues were based on erroneous assumptions about the other individual, which, when brought to light, proved to be misunderstandings. As the free exchange continued the emotion moved from negative to positive. The two owners soon developed a plan for repairing the harm they had caused by their inappropriate behavior, including informing their employees that the feud had ended.

Conferencing has been around for less than a decade, while workplace conferencing is still in its infancy. Anyone who has experienced the power of the process recognizes that it will change the way we do business.

CHAPTER 17

Avoiding Surprises

A facilitator, in preparing for the conference, tries to avoid surprises. The more one anticipates the issues that might arise, the better the conference is likely to be. Learning the details of the incident, talking with all the participants, building rapport, hearing what they think and feel, making personal visits whenever one feels that the victim or offender would benefit—those efforts can prevent unexpected problems in the conference.

Uncooperative Victim

Nonetheless, surprises happen. In the very first conference that I facilitated at an alternative school Roberto, the victim, surprised me. He had been threatened by Eddie, who was angry because Roberto had been allowed to play his choice of music in an activity period at the school. Despite the triviality of the dispute, Eddie ran out to the school van that transported Roberto and pounded on the van windows as the vehicle pulled away. The van driver reported that Eddie screamed and threatened that he would get the victim the next day.

The alternative school decided to discharge Eddie, whose behavior was spiraling downward, unless he agreed to a conference.

In my pre-conference discussion with Roberto, the victim said he wanted to confront Eddie but in the actual conference Roberto suddenly minimized the threats that had been made. One of Roberto's friends, there as a support person, was shocked. When he was asked how the incident affected him, he said that he thought it was very serious and was surprised that Roberto now made light of the threats. The victim's sudden change of heart undermined the effectiveness of the conference.

Eddie refused to offer an apology to Roberto as suggested by his family and friends. He claimed that he didn't do anything wrong. No one could persuade him otherwise and Roberto didn't even try. At that point I realized that Eddie was not even meeting the conference prerequisite of acknowledging that he had committed an offense, so I announced that I was ending the conference. Eddie was startled by my decision and stormed out into the hallway. Two students who came as his supporters asked if I would continue the conference if they could get Eddie to admit his wrongdoing. I agreed. They returned with a much more compliant Eddie who apologized and cooperated throughout the rest of the conference.

When I gave Roberto a ride home after the conference, I asked him if he was afraid of Eddie getting back at him. Roberto said that he wasn't afraid of that, but he had been thinking about all the crazy things he had done and fights he had caused when he was on drugs and just didn't feel right "making a big thing of it" when Eddie did it to him. We both agreed that Eddie, who had successfully completed a residential drug-and-alcohol treatment program some months before, had probably relapsed. I asked Roberto if he thought Eddie had been high during the conference. Roberto agreed that it certainly was possible.

The next day Eddie violated all the commitments he had made during the conference. He was discharged from the school. Obviously conferencing does not always positively influence behavior, especially when the offender is abusing drugs and alcohol. Eddie was sent back to a treatment program by his probation officer.

Conferencing is not a substitute for counseling, for drug-and-alcohol treatment or for other kinds of interventions and assessments. Rather, it is a narrowly defined way to replace arbitrary punishment for wrongdoing. That's all. The conference outcome is determined by the participants. Other recommendations or actions that professionals might propose for the offender are not the business of the conference. The participants may propose some of those same conditions for the offender. If the offender agrees and if there is funding available, then they may happen, but that is incidental to the primary purpose—for the offender and other conference participants to agree on how to remedy the harm that was done.

Other Offenses

On other occasions, as mentioned in an earlier story, other crimes may be reported by the offender. If the group is shocked or distracted by the offense, then the conference should be stopped. But if the offender is merely trying to "come clean" about other relatively minor offenses, like an old incident of shoplifting, the conference should proceed. If the offense that is mentioned warrants further attention, but not in the current conference, the facilitator may talk to the offender afterward. The offender is protected by the confidentiality of the conference, so the facilitator can only encourage a voluntary action on the part of the offender.

Routine Conference

Even a seemingly routine conference can surprise the facilitator. Two young boys, Paul and Steve, went into the home of a neighbor whose door was ajar and stole loose change. A neighbor saw the boys go into the house and told the boys' parents. Both sets of parents confronted their sons, who readily admitted the offense. The parents were extremely upset with their sons' behavior. Before they called the neighbors who were the victims, they called the local police to ask if an officer could give their children a lecture or something that would make an impression on the boys. The police officer told the parents that rather than a lecture, he would recommend a restorative conference if the victims were willing to participate. The couple whose home had been entered understood that these were only young boys who had taken some loose change. But they also appreciated that Paul's and Steve's parents wanted to appropriately set limits with their children and agreed to participate.

The conference was proceeding smoothly. The boys were completely remorseful. The parents could not have been more supportive of the victims. The victims could not have been more understanding or generous.

Then Paul, in a true act of contrition, said, "I'm really sorry about the pictures."

The pictures? The facilitator looked at the parents. What pictures? He looked at the victim couple who at first were puzzled, then concerned. He announced a "time out" in the conference and went out into the hall with the couple to talk.

The pictures in question were photos of the wife disrobed in various ways, taken by her husband. They had been hidden in their bedroom dresser. The boys had discovered the pictures, stolen them and showed them to their friends at school.

The facilitator was just as embarrassed as the couple, but when all regained their composure, the couple decided to proceed with the conference. The conference resumed its cooperative tone and reached a satisfactory conclusion. Those of us who plan to facilitate conferences are well reminded that even the most routine conference can produce unexpected twists and turns.

CHAPTER 18

Just the Facts

Many readers may remember police sergeant Joe Friday, played by Jack Webb on the long-running television program *Dragnet*. Sergeant Friday advised witnesses to give him "just the facts, ma'am, just the facts." Facts make the criminal justice system run. To prove the case in an adversarial system you must have the right facts. The facts related to a conference are significant to the extent they help the facilitator envision the conference, contact the right people, support the victim and prepare the offender to accept responsibility. Beginning facilitators may focus excessively on the facts. They read the court documentation but forget that making participants comfortable expressing their feelings is a better use of their energy. Conferences rely more on feelings than facts.

Onlooker at the Assault

Victims often accept even outright lies by offenders if their emotional needs are otherwise met. I facilitated a conference for a serious assault by six youths that occurred in the spring of their senior year at an urban Catholic high school. Ben, a well-intentioned young man in their neighborhood, tried to interest them in doing something more purposeful than drinking beer all evening at their favorite street corner. Not only were they not interested, but they beat him severely until he was rescued by a passerby.

By the time I became involved, about a year after the assault, most of the offenders had been dealt with through the courts. Totally frustrated with the insensitivity of the courts toward her son and her family, Ben's mother asked me if I would facilitate a restorative conference, even though three of the youths had been convicted and placed on probation. Ultimately one of the offenders, Randy, agreed to participate. Another, who had been convicted as an adult and ordered by the judge to participate in the conference, never showed up.

Two days before the conference I realized I had made a serious mistake. I had relied on the facts gathered by the police. Randy had stated he was remorseful for having been present at the assault and not having intervened to stop it. He claimed that he was an onlooker, not a participant. I foolishly assumed that Ben was aware of that police record and had accepted that view. When I mentioned Randy's involvement as an onlooker, Ben objected. He insisted that he distinctly remembered Randy as one of his assailants.

I was in a dilemma. The offender had not admitted the offense, so a key conference prerequisite was not met. Yet Ben wanted to proceed with the conference. I felt that I had to honor the victim. He seemed to fully understand that the only satisfaction he and his supporters might get from the conference was an opportunity to express their feelings. I called Ben's parents, his sister and her boyfriend, and others whom he had nominated as supporters. All were apprised of the less-than-ideal situation. All chose to attend. The morning of the conference I again approached Randy, who arrived at the conference with his father. I strongly suggested that if he had done the assault, this would be a good time and place to admit it, make amends and move on with his life. He was adamant that he had not hit the victim.

The conference began with Randy telling his version of the assault. He apologized for having anything to do with the assault and was willing to accept consequences for his involvement, but he again asserted that he was an onlooker and not a participant.

As he finished speaking Ben challenged him, claiming that he had a clear recollection of those individuals who had hit him. Other members of the family expressed their dismay and anger at Randy's resistance to admitting his involvement. When Ben's father referred to the offender as a liar, Randy's father angrily came to his son's defense. That was the only time that I had to intervene in what was a very emotional exchange. I said that it was important that we not call each other names. I reminded everyone that we were here to find out how people have been affected by the incident and how to repair the harm that it caused. Both angry fathers nodded and the conference proceeded emotionally, but without further verbal abuse.

The detective who investigated the assault played an important role in the conference. He was well-regarded by both Ben's and Randy's group. At one point in the conference, he said that Randy's father, when informed of his son's involvement in the assault, immediately asked about the well-being of the victim. This softened the anger of Ben's group.

The detective also supported Ben's version of the assault. He emphasized that he found Ben to be an accurate observer. When he made the initial arrests, even in a street setting with a crowd of teen-agers, he was confident that he was apprehending the correct suspect because of Ben's precise and detailed description of each offender. For that reason, he explained, he was inclined to trust the victim's recollection of who had hit him.

Ben's group tried to persuade Randy to recant and admit his involvement in the assault, assuring him that they were not interested in vengeance, just the truth. Given that Randy's version of events differed from Ben's, I was reluctant to limit the discussion and leave the victim and his supporters feeling that they had not had an adequate opportunity to pursue their concerns. The discussion continued for almost an hour.

Suddenly the victim group seemed to shift their mood. Ben and his supporters collectively realized that for over a year Randy had been telling the police and his parents that he had only been an onlooker in the assault. If he were lying, as Ben insisted he was, Randy was so deeply invested in his lie that he wasn't going to tell the truth now.

Although Randy would not admit that he had hit Ben, he claimed that if he had it to do over again he would have tried to stop the assault or run for help. He agreed that he should have done that when the assault began. He also agreed to do community service as a way of making amends for his involvement. And he apologized.

After the conference Ben told me that he accepted that the offender would never admit the facts of the incident. He said what the conference achieved for him was to put closure on the most traumatic event of his life. However imperfect the conference, it met his underlying emotional needs.

For several centuries and until recently, the evolution of human thought has emphasized intellect and reason. Our culture has disparaged emotion as a weakness, an unpleasant reality that humans should strive to overcome with thoughtfulness and intelligence.

The tide is beginning to turn. We have begun to see the role emotion plays in our lives. Daniel Goleman, longtime science writer for *The New York Times*, said that "emotional intelligence" is a far better predictor of success and well-being than intellectual intelligence. Goleman's landmark book, *Emotional Intelligence*, says that our ability to empathize, to understand and appreciate the emotional needs of others is a key element of emotional intelligence. Conferencing fosters precisely that ability.

Racial Bias

A conference dealing with a high school racial incident highlights the contrast between the current legal system's focus on facts and the Real Justice emphasis on emotion. Two girls were cutting class. They went out to the school parking lot and found an unlocked car in which to smoke cigarettes. They must have known that the car they entered belonged to one of the few African-American students in the school. They wrote the words "Nigger" and "KKK" and drew a Nazi swastika on the upholstery and ceiling of the vehicle. They also burned holes in the seats and the dashboard with their cigarettes and the car's cigarette lighter.

Angel, the girl who owned the car, was devastated. Not only had her car been vandalized, but the racist graffiti made the incident especially painful. The girls were caught and admitted the vandalism. They explained that they were only trying to bring attention to the problem of racial bias in their high school. Despite their seemingly ridiculous claim, Angel wanted to handle the offense as a conference rather than wait for it to work slowly through the courts. She wanted to confront the offenders with her feelings and then put the incident behind her. Like the offender in the previously cited assault case, the two girls held to their story but readily expressed remorse. They agreed to community service work and to publicly apologize to the student body for having brought the negative publicity to the high school and for having offended many students who cared about Angel.

When the girls apologized in the conference, Angel told them that she knew they were not telling the truth about why they vandalized her car. Yet she accepted their apology and acknowledged that they were genuinely sorry for what they did.

If we feel frustrated with a conferencing process that tolerates such factual inaccuracies by offenders in the assault and vandalism cases, we might ask ourselves why it's a problem and whose problem it is. If the need for a perfect recitation of the facts gets in the way, why obstruct healing? For victims in both cases, conferencing brought closure and allowed them to move on with their lives.

Passive Offender

I saw a videotape that vividly illustrated this conflict between facts and feelings. The video showed an encounter between one of two offenders and the mother and father of a teen-age girl who was abducted, raped and shot to death. The offender, a dull man apparently easily influenced by the other offender, was remorseful and anxious to make amends. He claimed that the other offender had forced him to participate in the crime at gunpoint, which was probably largely true, especially when the girl was first abducted. The father, who had visited the crime scene, asked the offender why he didn't try to help his daughter or save himself at various intervals that night, particularly when it would have been easy to suddenly run into the thick dark woods. The offender was unwilling to acknowledge that he had had any options.

The father later told those who observed the video that he could not fully accept this offender's story. He was certain that the offender had been more of a participant in the crime than he was willing to admit. The father speculated that the offender could not bring himself to face the truth and might actually believe he had played only a passive role. Sadly, I thought, the only one who could have honestly reported the truth was the victim.

The father explained that he and his wife had accepted that the facts of the crime will not be known, that the truth will remain ambiguous. As parents they faced the offenders, voiced their outrage and their grief, gained the understanding they could and then put closure on the greatest tragedy parents can experience. For their own sake and for the well-being of their surviving daughter, they had to address their emotional needs and, like the victims of the assault and the racial incident, try to move on.

Despite Sergeant Friday's assertion, justice is not "just the facts." Our criminal justice system fails to repair the harm caused by crime, because it fails to acknowledge feelings. Justice is not about evidence, proof, witnesses, convictions or punishment. Real Justice can be achieved when we address the emotional needs of all who have been affected by a crime.

CHAPTER 19

Community

Community is a carelessly used word. We use the word, generally without clarification, to refer to our neighborhood, our region, our colleagues, our world. What we do know about community is that we seem to have lost it. Most of us in the modern world do not feel as connected to others around us as our parents or grandparents did in their time.

Lack of connectedness with others is usually found in young offenders. We should not be surprised. Our society inhibits the development of relationships in many ways.

Families stand alone as supposedly self-sufficient units comprised of a mother, a father and their children. They try to cope with the stresses and struggles of life without the network of extended family that provided mutual support and protection in previous generations.

Half of the nuclear families in the baby-boomer generation broke apart at least once. Children of divorced families often lack trust in the durability of human relationships.

Isolation from extended family often results from our moving from place to place. Some parents' careers demand a move every two or three years. These families may never build lasting relationships with others in their neighborhoods and schools. Many people do not even know their next-door neighbors.

As our institutions grow larger they become more impersonal. After World War II, public schools throughout North America were consolidated into larger administrative units. In the interest of improving school facilities, rural and small-town schools were closed and large regional institutions were created. But what was gained in consolidation was lost in other ways. Many students who now feel alone and adrift in large schools would benefit from the personal attention and camaraderie of a smaller school. That same trend toward bigness and depersonalization is exemplified by the growth of superstores, multinational corporations, big governments and sprawling suburbs.

Government agencies have tried many initiatives to foster a sense of community. But government itself is not community. "Community policing," one of the most widespread initiatives of the criminal justice system, typically involves an administrative decision to create a storefront police substation or shift police from riding in cars to foot patrol or riding on bicycles. The police administration usually does not involve citizens in the decision making or implementation, so there is rarely a sense of connection or ownership that develops. Official efforts that carry the "community" label usually produce superficial results because government sees community as simply part of its geographic jurisdiction.

Defining Community

Community is not a place. Rather, it is a feeling, a perception. When people see themselves as belonging to a community, they feel connected. They have a sense of ownership and responsibility. They feel that they have a say in how things are run and a stake in the outcome. Conferencing creates a sense of ownership and connectedness between people. It can help renew our feeling of community.

The conferencing process fosters involvement and ownership. Conferencing engages people at the outset by asking them to make choices. In preparing for the conference, the facilitator respectfully invites everyone to participate on a voluntary basis. People have to decide whether they are willing to attend. Even offenders, faced with the threat of more formal disciplinary or legal processes, have a choice. They can, and sometimes do, refuse to participate in the conference. Again, at the beginning of the conference, participants are reminded that participation is their choice. They can leave at any time.

The conference provides each participant with an opportunity to speak. Not only is each individual asked a series of open-ended questions, but the facilitator later checks to see if anyone has more to say. Most significantly all of the conference participants have a say in the outcome. They decide how to repair the harm caused by the offender. Rarely in our society are individuals treated with such respect.

The term "micro-community" has been used to describe the relationship between those who are brought together in a conference. Initially, the common bond that the participants share is the offense. By the end of the process they also share the experience of the conference itself, an emotional event that forges relationships between participants. Long after the conference those relationships will be quietly acknowledged by a wave or a knowing smile whenever participants encounter one another. Police officers have often told me how an offender from a conference they facilitated now waves when they see each other on the streets.

Government Interference

Some government officials, confusing the concept of community with their own geographic jurisdiction, have suggested that government-appointed "community representatives" attend each conference. Such community representatives hinder the conference process because they lack real emotional involvement with the offender, the victim or the incident. They bring little to the conference that cannot be provided by those who have an emotional stake in the incident, and they often convey righteousness and moral superiority that dampens the free expression of emotion by the other participants.

I fear that government will interfere with the gradual spread of conferencing in North America by trying to legislate and regulate conferencing, rather than letting it be adopted as a grassroots innovation in each jurisdiction. To date, conferencing has been implemented in schools and police departments and court systems when there is enough local support for the concept. It requires no formal legislative action, only guidelines as to what range of situations can be conferenced. Those of us who marvel at the power of this simple and elegant process hope that it will never be compromised and complicated by the heavy hand of government.

In New Zealand, conferencing was invented by legislation, not through experimentation. Some experienced facilitators in that country have expressed their frustration with the rigid legal and bureaucratic requirements imposed on their process by politicians and administrators who have no direct experience with conferencing. These New Zealand facilitators see some significant advantages in the Wagga Wagga conferencing model that Terry O'Connell developed through trial and error, but they may not adopt that approach.

Ironically, similar political and bureaucratic constraints have ended conferencing by police officers in Wagga Wagga and the rest of the state of New South Wales. Politicians and the administration of the large police force that serves the entire state have ruled against police officers doing conferences, despite the compelling evidence provided by two excellent Australian research studies that support the merits of police conferencing.

Only when we have a depth of experience with conferencing and the process is thoroughly understood and supported by both practitioners and the populace should we consider legislation. Issues such as protecting the confidentiality of information brought to light in conferences would benefit from legislative clarification, but we need to allow the innovation to mature before we pass laws about it.

In many instances government need not be involved at all. In Vermont, representatives of the Department of Corrections and other government officials have been discussing "community justice centers," which would provide, among other things, a supervised pool of screened and trained volunteers to run conferences as needed for police, schools, courts and corrections. A retailer who catches a young shoplifter, for example, might opt to take the culprit directly to the community justice center for a conference without involving the police.

Community Empowerment

At this point the community justice center is only in the "brainstorming" phase of development, but if you think the idea is far-fetched, consider the following story. A youth vandalized a neighborhood tree house and stole a television set that he found there. When he was discovered and admitted his offense, the police advised the families in the neighborhood that they would like to handle the case as a restorative conference. By the time the police officer handling the case began to contact families, he discovered that the neighbors and their children had gotten together with the offender and his family and had successfully run their own restorative conference. One of the neighbors had previously attended a restorative conference for a different matter and felt confident that he could run the conference. So instead of waiting for the police, the neighbors "took the law into their own hands." Unlike vigilantes seeking vengeance, the neighborhood used restorative justice, which repairs the harm and allows the offender to be reintegrated in the community.

Kay Pranis, restorative justice planner for the Minnesota Department of Corrections, suggests that restorative justice requires a partnership between government and community in which government is responsible for legality while the community provides morality. The government has the responsibility for oversight and must ensure that the process and outcome stay within the bounds of law. The community can convey a unique sense of right and wrong, based not on fear of punishment, but based on a feeling of mutual regard for others with whom one feels connected. Conferencing done in the right spirit by citizens themselves, as exemplified by the neighbors who handled the tree-house incident on their own, can build healthier communities.

The Royal Canadian Mounted Police have adopted conferencing for juvenile offenses as a community policing initiative. But the RCMP is focusing its efforts on training police officers to teach community volunteers how to facilitate conferences. Then police officers will process cases and refer them to the community to facilitate.

Government cannot do it all. We need to recognize the limits of laws and police and courts and prisons and the critical need for a sense of community. Conferencing can help move us in that direction by turning wrongdoing into an opportunity to build community.

Ice Fishing

One winter night a group of teen-age boys vandalized several recreational ice-fishing houses. The structures, which were set up on the frozen surface of a local lake every year, sheltered the fishermen from the extreme cold. Some of these houses, which were quite substantial, even providing sleeping and cooking facilities.

Although the offenders were identified, the public prosecutor felt he could not proceed with the case because he did not have enough information to charge each offender with specific damage to a specific ice-fishing house. Instead, the local police handled the case with one large restorative conference.

Henry, one of the owners, was particularly upset that the offenders were not going to court. He and his son, Henry Jr., now an adult, had spent many years fishing on the lake. Their ice-fishing house had evolved into an elaborate structure. The house was seriously damaged. Henry wanted the culprits punished. He angrily warned that he would not be satisfied with the conference.

The night of the conference the offenders and their parents met the victims and their families. Although all lived in the same suburb, few in the victims' and offenders' groups knew each other.

The facilitator asked each of the youths to tell what had happened. Each youth individually admitted his part in the vandalism and expressed remorse for his actions.

Then the owners and their family members were asked to tell how the vandalism had affected them. The facilitator avoided asking Henry, the angriest owner, to speak first. When it was Henry's turn he chose not to speak. Henry Jr., however, spoke eloquently about how he and his father had built and refined their ice-fishing house over the years and how it represented the happy memories of those times he and his father had spent together. His comments touched the hearts of everyone at the conference and conveyed the realization that the ice-fishing houses were more than shelters to their owners.

The conference proceeded smoothly through the agreement phase. The young offenders appropriately apologized and they or their parents paid for the damages that night, while still at the conference. When the facilitator asked if anyone had anything further to say, Henry indicated that he wanted to speak.

"I know it may seem strange, but I want to thank you boys for what you've done. I was very angry with you, and I wasn't happy about this conference. But if none of this had happened, I might never have heard my son talk about how much all those years of fishing and working together meant to him. So I want to thank you for giving me that opportunity."

Then Henry looked around the room at all of the offenders and said, "I'd also like to invite all of you boys and your fathers, as soon as the damage is repaired, to come ice fishing with us."

CHAPTER 20

Conclusion

We, as citizens, must help revolutionize our society's response to wrongdoing. We cannot wait for the politicians to find a new strategy. Though they claim to be our leaders, they seem to follow trends rather than set them.

In the decade between 1986 and 1996 the American prison population more than doubled, from 744,208 to 1,630,940. The Bureau of Justice Statistics projects another 51 percent increase in the prison population by the year 2000. No other industrial nation in the world has incarcerated such a large percentage of its population; yet many other countries have lower crime rates.

Our schools are experiencing more disciplinary problems, more violence, truancy and dropouts. While American schools fine parents for their children's truancy and adopt "zero tolerance" policies, which suspend and expel more students, the negative statistics grow.

Victims are revictimized by our current processes. Offenses are defined as violations against the state or the school, so criminal justice and school discipline fail to repair the harm done to individuals and communities. Scant attention is paid to healing. The focus is on punishment.

Relying on punishment in courts and schools, we stigmatize offenders and create outcasts. Punishment does not foster understanding and empathy for victims; it fosters resentment and alienation. How ironic that offenders see themselves as victims.

In the criminal justice system, particularly, we are inconsistent. Courts are so overwhelmed that they often minimize offenses with plea bargaining and probation, without appropriately confronting offenders or making them repair the harm they have done to their victims.

We need a system of justice that holds offenders accountable for their actions and provides meaningful consequences. Offenders must face what they have done and those they have harmed. Certainly there are offenders who are so dangerous that they must be confined, but we are incarcerating far too many, wasting money and ruining lives. We need to look at our dilemma with cool clear eyes. Let us abandon slogans like "if you do the crime, you do the time" and reassess our failed policies. If things are not getting better, common sense dictates that we do something different. Real Justice is different.

We can raise our voices as citizens and voters. Through letters to the editor, talk radio, other public forums and at the ballot box, we can tell judges and legislators and governors and school boards to support the development of conferencing. And we can sing the praises of those who already have done so. As employers and supervisors and employees, we can encourage conferencing in the workplace. As police, attorneys, judges, probation, parole and corrections officers we can open ourselves and the criminal justice system to conferencing. As educators and academicians and administrators, we can foster conferencing in our classrooms and schools. As parents, we can support conferencing in schools, day-care centers, camps, church groups, scout troops and other youth organizations. We can volunteer to be trained and facilitate conferences.

In the many years since I went to juvenile court for the Uncle Marty's Sneaker Barn burglary, I have never been so hopeful about meaningful reform as I am now. The road to real justice will be long and difficult, but I am encouraged by the people who have responded enthusiastically and decided to make the journey with us.

Of course, there are still skeptics. Even when we cite the favorable research results achieved to date, naysayers raise new fears and objections. We suggest that they observe a conference. When they do, as many skeptics have, their objections will melt away. They become advocates.

For me, my intuition was the critical factor in deciding to create the Real Justice program. While I acknowledge the value of research, I know that conferencing will gain momentum and become an established practice, not as a result of scientific evaluation, but because it feels right. In the closing hours of a three-day restorative justice seminar in Washington, D.C., some of the participants expressed the need for more research to evaluate processes like conferencing. In the midst of the discussion an elder Native American gentleman rose to speak. He looked around the group, shaking his head and smiling, then spoke slowly.

"You don't have to do research to prove that it works. You just have to do it. And then, if the sun seems to shine a little brighter, you'll know that it works."

Epilogue

Much has happened since 1997 when I wrote the Real Justice book. Real Justice and its licensees around the world have trained thousands of people to facilitate restorative conferences. Schools, community agencies, youth programs, police, courts, prisons and businesses have used the formal restorative conference to respond to crime and wrongdoing.

We have been challenged by the sobering fact that meaningful change is difficult to achieve and even harder to sustain. Nonetheless, restorative conferences and related restorative practices, such as sentencing circles, family group conferences and family group decision making for child protection and family violence, are gradually spreading. Importantly, we began to realize that restorative justice could readily be incorporated informally into people's daily lives, beyond the use of formal processes. In the surveys conducted by the Real Justice program following our early trainings, we learned that while most of our trainees had not facilitated a formal conference, many were using the language and underlying principles of restorative conferencing. Educators who had been trained, instead of handing out punishments, began to address incidents of school wrongdoing by getting students to think about what they had done, whom they had affected and how they might repair the harm they had caused. Real Justice trainees, in parenting their own children, were conducting informal restorative conferences.

We developed the "Social Discipline Window" (see Figure 3) to describe our new understanding of restorative strategies. Those who use only high control in response to wrongdoing, but provide little support, are "punitive." Their leadership style is "authoritarian" because they primarily do things TO people. Those who only respond to wrongdoing with high support and little control are "permissive." Their leadership style is "paternalistic" because they primarily do things FOR people. The neglectful leader who does NOT do anything in response to wrongdoing is simply "irresponsible."

THE SOCIAL DISCIPLINE WINDOW
Figure 3

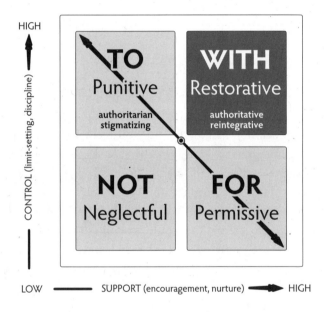

Those who respond to wrongdoing with both high control and high support are "restorative." Their leadership style is "authoritative" because they do things WITH people. Although they have authority, they engage and empower people, allowing them to be heard and to have a say in the outcome.

.   We developed the "Restorative Practices Continuum" (see
Figure 4) to describe the range of possible restorative approaches.
Beginning with the most informal practices on the left side of the
continuum, the affective statement simply expresses emotion, telling wrongdoers how their behavior has affected the speaker. The
affective question asks wrongdoers to reflect on how their behavior
has affected others. The small impromptu conference is spontaneous, without the preparation associated with the formal conference.
Circles and groups are somewhat more formal but still less structured than the restorative conference itself.

THE RESTORATIVE PRACTICES CONTINUUM
Figure 4 .

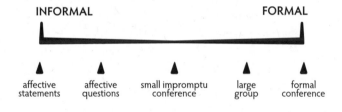

As restorative practices move from informal to formal, they
tend to involve more people, take more time to carry out, require
more preparation and are more structured. They also tend to have
more impact.

.   We began to use the term "restorative practices" because we
realized that restorative justice is only one of many areas of human
activity that can benefit from a restorative approach. It is also relevant to education, social work, psychology, counseling, parenting,
organizational leadership—anything that involves the management and motivation of human beings and the need to establish
social discipline.

The fundamental thesis underlying restorative practices is that people are happier, more productive, more cooperative and more likely to make positive changes when those in authority do things WITH them, rather than TO them or FOR them.

We also began to think in terms of proactive and reactive restorative practices. Not only can restorative practices be used to react to wrongdoing, but also their deliberate use before there is any wrongdoing fosters emotional bonds and builds relationships. Using circles, for example, in classroom or business settings, encourages people to express their feelings and personal stories, allowing them to get to know each other and creating a sense of community.

In 1999 I founded the International Institute for Restorative Practices (IIRP), a nonprofit educational organization, to take over the ongoing Real Justice program and several new programs that were created to spread restorative practices. SaferSanerSchools[TM] brings restorative practices to education, Family Power[SM] addresses social work and counseling, and Good Company[SM] focuses on organizational management. The IIRP collaborates with the Community Service Foundation and Buxmont Academy, two nonprofit organizations that provide educational, counseling and residential services for delinquent and at-risk youth in eastern Pennsylvania (csfbuxmont.org) and which serve as demonstration programs for the use of restorative practices.

The international conferences about restorative practices that began under the auspices of the Real Justice program in 1998 in North America are now run by the IIRP and are held on several continents at more frequent intervals. The IIRP has produced a variety of new educational resources about restorative practices, including several websites (iirp.org, realjustice.org, safersaner-schools.org, familypower.org and goodcompanyonline.org) and an email publication called the Restorative Practices eForum, which has thousands of subscribers throughout the world.

We have established program branches of the IIRP in several countries: IIRP UK, IIRP Canada, Real Justice Australia and the

Community Service Foundation of Hungary. We also have Real Justice licensees in China, Costa Rica, the Netherlands, New Zealand, Sweden, Thailand and in many locations in the United States and Canada.

In 2006 the Pennsylvania Department of Education authorized the IIRP as a specialized research and graduate degree–granting institution, the first graduate school in the world wholly dedicated to restorative practices.

The IIRP is dedicated to building a global alliance that fosters the use of restorative practices across professional and national boundaries. We invite you to join us.

— Ted Wachtel, 2007

References

Braithwaite, J. (1989). *Crime, shame and reintegration*. Cambridge, UK: Cambridge University Press.

Moore, D.B. (1997). Pride, shame and empathy in peer relations: New theory and practice in education and juvenile justice. In K. Rigby & P. Slee (Eds.), *Children's peer relations*. London: Routledge.

Moore, D.B. & Forsythe, L. (1995). *A new approach to juvenile justice: An evaluation of restorative conferencing in Wagga Wagga*. A report to the Criminology Research Council, Wagga Wagga, New South Wales, Australia: Centre for Rural Social Research, Charles Sturt University-Riverina.

Nathanson, D.L. (1992). *Shame and pride: Affect, sex and the birth of the self*. New York: Norton & Company.

National Organization for Victim Assistance Newsletter (1997), Vol. 17, No. 11.

Zehr, H. (1990). *Changing lenses: A new focus for crime and justice*. Scottdale, PA: Herald Press.

Conferencing Handbook

The Real Justice® Training Manual

by
Terry O'Connell
Ben Wachtel
Ted Wachtel

About This Manual

This manual is a procedural guide to facilitating Real Justice conferences. It focuses on lesser incidents of wrongdoing, the vast majority of offenses. This manual will not, by itself, prepare readers to facilitate a conference for serious offenses involving severe trauma for victims.

Real Justice provides training using this manual as a resource. However, the manual is available to anyone, and its use in a training does not signify that Real Justice is affiliated with that training.

CHAPTER 1

The Script

A conference is a forum where people deal with wrongdoing and conflict. All participants can speak, express their feelings and, most importantly, have a say in the outcome. A conference is a democratic experience in which those most affected by a problem decide how to respond to it.

The conference facilitator brings the participants together, creates a safe and supportive environment, keeps the process focused and records the decisions of the group. The conference facilitator does *not* make or influence the decisions, but lets participants express themselves and find their own creative solutions. The best conference facilitators guide the process, yet remain in the background. They encourage, but do not control or dictate.

The script is the heart of the conference. It is a simple, reliable tool that allows a facilitator to run a conference successfully without extensive mediation or counseling training. First the script prescribes a series of open-ended questions that encourage people to respond "affectively," that is, to express how they were affected by the issue that brought them together. Next the script provides participants an opportunity to exchange ideas, develop a plan to address the conflict or wrongdoing, and repair the harm that resulted. Finally the script invites participants to an informal, postconference social gathering, when refreshments are served and participants mingle and talk.

Please read the "Conference Facilitator's Script" on the next four pages now. (Facilitators can photocopy this script for their use in running conferences or download from www.realjustice.org/pdf/script.pdf.)

Origins of the Script

The script for conferencing originated with one of the authors of this manual, Terry O'Connell, a community policing sergeant in Wagga Wagga, New South Wales, Australia, in 1991.

Conferencing began two years earlier in New Zealand as part of the Children, Youth and Families Act of 1989. That legislation stemmed from discontent among the Maori, the indigenous people of New Zealand, with the way courts dealt with their young people in criminal and social welfare matters. After convening a commission to study the problem, the government decided that a wide range of juvenile justice offenses and child welfare cases would be dealt with through a process called a "family group conference." Instead of going to court, the government would bring together the extended family of a child or youth to develop a plan to address the problem. Although the new process applied to all New Zealand children and youth, it reflected the Maori tradition that the individual's family and community should be directly involved in any response to wrongdoing and conflict, a practice typical of most aboriginal or indigenous people.

CONFERENCE FACILITATOR'S SCRIPT

Download printable version: www.realjustice.org/pdf/script.pdf

1. PREAMBLE

"**Welcome. As you know, my name is** (your name) **and I will be facilitating this conference.**"

Now introduce each conference participant and state his/her relationship to the offender/s or victim/s.

"**Thank you all for attending. I know that this is difficult for all of you, but your presence will help us deal with the matter that has brought us together. This is an opportunity for all of you to be involved in repairing the harm that has been done.**"

"**This conference will focus on an incident that happened** (state the date, place and nature of offense without elaborating)**. It is important to understand that we will focus on what** (offender name/s) **did and how that unacceptable behavior has affected others. We are not here to decide whether** (offender name/s) **is**/are **good or bad. We want to explore in what way people have been affected and hopefully work toward repairing the harm that has resulted. Does everyone understand this?**"

"(Offender name/s) **has**/have **admitted his**/her/their **part in the incident.**"

Say to offender/s: "**I must tell you that you do not have to participate in this conference and are free to leave at**

any time, as is anyone else. If you do leave, the matter may be referred to court/handled by the school disciplinary policy/handled in another way**."**

"This matter, however, may be finalized if you participate in a positive manner and comply with the conference agreement."

Say to offender/s: **"Do you understand?"**

2. OFFENDER/S
"We'll start with (one of offenders' names)**."**

If there is more than one offender, have each respond to all of the following questions.

> **"What happened?"**
> **"What were you thinking about at the time?"**
> **"What have you thought about since the incident?"**
> **"Who do you think has been affected by your actions?"**
> **"How have they been affected?"**

3. VICTIM/S
If there is more than one victim, have each respond to all of the following questions.

> **"What was your reaction at the time of the incident?"**
> **"How do you feel about what happened?"**
> **"What has been the hardest thing for you?"**
> **"How did your family and friends react when they heard about the incident?"**

4. VICTIM SUPPORTERS

Have each respond to all of the following questions.

> **"What did you think when you heard about the incident?"**
> **"How do you feel about what happened?"**
> **"What has been the hardest thing for you?"**
> **"What do you think are the main issues?"**

5. OFFENDER SUPPORTERS

To parent/caregiver ask: **"This has been difficult for you, hasn't it? Would you like to tell us about it?"**

Have each respond to all of the following questions.

> **"What did you think when you heard about the incident?"**
> **"How do you feel about what happened?"**
> **"What has been the hardest thing for you?"**
> **"What do you think are the main issues?"**

6. OFFENDER/S

Ask the offender/s: **"Is there anything you want to say at this time?"**

7. REACHING AN AGREEMENT

Ask the victim/s: **"What would you like from today's conference?"**

Ask the offender/s to respond.

At this point, the participants discuss what should be in the final agreement. Solicit comments from participants.

It is important that you ask the offender/s to respond to each suggestion before the group moves to the next suggestion, asking **"What do you think about that?"** Then determine that the offender/s agree/s before moving on. Allow for negotiation.

As the agreement develops, clarify each item and make the written document as specific as possible, including details, deadlines and follow-up arrangements.

As you sense that the agreement discussion is drawing to a close, say to the participants: **"Before I prepare the written agreement, I'd like to make sure that I have accurately recorded what has been decided."**

Read the items in the agreement aloud and look to the participants for acknowledgment. Make any necessary corrections.

8. CLOSING THE CONFERENCE

"Before I formally close this conference, I would like to provide everyone with a final opportunity to speak. Is there anything anyone wants to say?"

Allow for participants to respond, and when they are done, say: **"Thank you for your contributions in dealing with this difficult matter. Congratulations on the way you have worked through the issues. Please help yourselves to some refreshments while I prepare the agreement."**

Allow participants ample time to have refreshments and interact. The informal period after the formal conference is very important.

New Zealand's bold experiment in empowering families to take greater responsibility for their own children has influenced philosophy and practice among social workers and criminal justice professionals throughout the world. Among those influenced was Terry O'Connell, who was working with a local committee of citizens in Wagga Wagga to develop new responses to juvenile crime. After exploring the idea, the citizen group decided to implement conferencing in their community.

Never having seen an actual conference, O'Connell improvised. He borrowed the concept and kept the name "family group conference," but changed the procedure substantially when he adapted it as a community policing response to juvenile offenses. Having a police officer facilitate the conference, rather than a social worker, was distinctly different from the New Zealand approach. O'Connell also wrote a script for the facilitator to follow, which simplified conducting conferences and helped ensure a reliable result.

The Wagga Wagga model of conferencing also gave the victim's family and friends a chance to be involved, unlike the original New Zealand process. New Zealand has since changed its law to provide victim supporters a role in family group conference (FGC) criminal cases. Another significant difference was that the New Zealand legislation prescribes an opportunity for the family of the child to "caucus," that is, to meet separately with only family members present, excluding social workers, police and others from being in the room. The government representatives can subsequently overrule the decision of the family, but only if the plan is deemed "impracticable or inconsistent with the principles" of the legislation. The caucus is not part of the scripted conference process developed by O'Connell. (The caucus associated with FGC — which is also part of family group decision making, or FGDM, the North American term — is now referred to as "family alone time" or "private family time" by practitioners.)

The Wagga Wagga conference model was a carefully orchestrated emotional encounter between young offenders, their victims and their respective friends and families, which typically resulted in a written plan to repair the harm caused by the offense. When victims and other conference participants began singing the praises of conferencing, the practice spread. The Australian media started reporting about conferences. Australian educators began using the process with incidents of school misconduct in 1994. Young offenders, if they agreed to participate, were diverted from the normal court or school disciplinary procedures.

In 1994 a Winston Churchill Fellowship enabled O'Connell to travel and tell others about his work with family group conferencing, which had come to be called by various names, including "community accountability conferencing," "diversionary conferencing," simply "conferencing" and "restorative conferencing." His trip fostered the adoption of conferencing by police and others in the United States, Canada and the United Kingdom.

During this trip, Ted Wachtel, a coauthor of this manual, heard O'Connell speak at a Bucks County Juvenile Court luncheon in Doylestown, Pennsylvania. Wachtel was then executive director of the Community Service Foundation, a nonprofit agency providing counseling, education and residential services to troubled and delinquent youth in southeastern Pennsylvania. After hearing O'Connell speak, Wachtel decided to found Real Justice, an international nonprofit program dedicated to fostering the use of the scripted model of conferencing and related restorative practices throughout the world.

Variations on the Script

When Real Justice began in 1994, conferencing addressed only juvenile offenses and school discipline issues. Conferencing is now used for a wide range of offenses in communities, schools, college campuses, institutions and workplaces. The script presented in this chapter is specifically for conferences dealing with criminal offenses and incidents of wrongdoing where offenders have admitted responsibility for the act and there is an identifiable victim.

Conferencing can also be used for truancy, drug possession and other "victimless" offenses, probation and parole violations, and interpersonal conflicts. It can sometimes be used when responsibility for an offense is not clear, but the parties affected are willing to participate in a conference. This handbook focuses on conferencing for incidents involving distinct victims and offenders, but the conference script and preparation can be modified to address other types of offenses, conflicts and situations, including school truancy or "victimless" offenses. Sometimes family and friends of offenders are embarrassed and concerned by the offender's actions and therefore indirectly victimized.

Silvan Tomkins's Affect Theory

Silvan Tomkins's psychological theory of human affect, as articulated by Donald Nathanson (1992), helps explain why the scripted conference is so effective.

Conferencing encourages free expression of affect, the biological basis for emotion and feeling. The conference allows expression of true feelings, while minimizing negative affect and maximizing positive affect. In Tomkins's theory, this kind of environment is the ideal setting for healthy human relationships.

The conference script uses open-ended questions that encourage the display of all nine basic affects (see Figure 1), which Tomkins identified as existing in every human being. Tomkins presented most affects as hyphenated word pairs that name the least and most intensive expressions of that affect. When a conference begins, people are feeling *disgust, dissmell* (which originated biologically as a response to offensive odor), *anger-rage, distress-anguish, fear-terror* and *shame-humiliation*. These six negative affects are the most prevalent when participants first enter the conference room and sit nervously as the conference begins.

When participants respond to the scripted questions, they may express any or all of those negative affects or feelings. Anger, distress, fear and shame are diminished through sharing. Their expression helps to reduce their intensity.

THE NINE AFFECTS
Figure 1

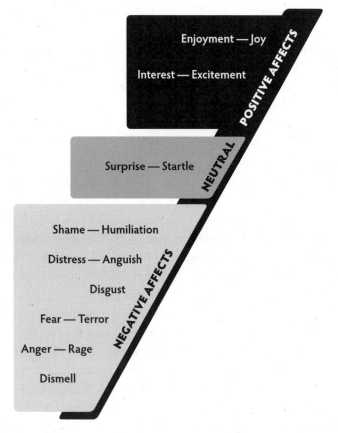

ADAPTED FROM NATHANSON, 1992

As the conference proceeds people experience a transition characterized by the neutral affect of *surprise-startle*. Victims, offenders and their supporters are usually surprised by what people say in the conference and how much better they begin to feel. When the conference reaches the agreement phase, participants are usually expressing the positive affects of *interest-excitement* and *enjoyment-joy*.

People recognize the affects seen on others' faces and tend to respond with the same affect. When one is angry, others become angry. When one feels better and smiles, so do others. Tomkins called this "affective resonance" or empathy. Through affective resonance, conference participants make the emotional journey together, feeling each other's feelings as they travel from anger and distress and shame to interest and enjoyment.

The prospective conference facilitator can take comfort in knowing that Tomkins's affect theory is reliably demonstrated by the scripted conference process. People consistently move from negative to positive feelings in the safe and structured environment created by the script.

Reintegrative Shaming

Tomkins teaches us that shame is a basic affect occurring spontaneously in all human beings when confronted about their wrongdoing. John Braithwaite, in *Crime, Shame and Reintegration* (1989), advises that the experience of dealing with shame should be reintegrative, not stigmatizing.

Braithwaite's sociological theory of "reintegrative shaming" suggests that Western society's current strategies for responding to crime and wrongdoing may actually be doing more harm than good. Schools and courts punish and humiliate offenders without offering a way to make amends, right the wrong or shed their "offender" label. Instead, offenders are stigmatized, alienated and pushed into society's growing negative subcultures. They join the others in their school or community who feel excluded from the mainstream and become a source of persistent trouble.

Braithwaite says societies that reintegrate offenders back into the community have a lower crime rate than those that stigmatize and alienate wrongdoers. Reintegration involves *separating the deed from the doer* so that society clearly disapproves of the crime or inappropriate behavior, but acknowledges the intrinsic worth of the individual. The conference script emphasizes that distinction by stating that, "It is important to understand that we will focus on what (offender name/s) did and how that unacceptable behavior has affected others. We are not here to decide whether (offender name/s) is/are good or bad."

In several ways, the conference script helps offenders move beyond their shame toward reintegration. The script provides an opportunity for offenders to take responsibility for their behavior and to apologize. In the agreement phase of the conference, offenders can define specific steps to repair the harm and show good faith, such as making restitution and doing community service. Finally the informal social interaction after the intense conference proceedings brings participants a sense of relief and allows them to interact one-to-one. Victims and offenders and their respective supporters often make gestures of reconciliation during this period, talking, sharing refreshments, shaking hands and sometimes even embracing.

Nathanson's Compass of Shame

Donald Nathanson's "compass of shame" clarifies how people react to and express their shame (see Figure 2.) They usually react with one or more of four general patterns or "scripts," which Nathanson depicts as directions on a compass: *attack other, attack self, withdrawal* and *avoidance.*

When parents or their offending children blame and criticize the school or the police officer when confronted with an offense, they illustrate the *attack other* response. These parents or offenders try to avoid shame by putting the responsibility on others. This is the most common response to shame exhibited in today's culture. Another contemporary response is *avoidance*, through alcohol, drug abuse or thrill-seeking behavior, like joy-riding in a stolen car.

THE COMPASS OF SHAME
Figure 2

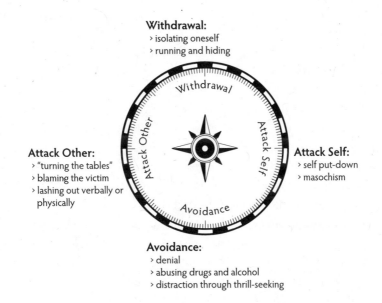

Withdrawal:
> isolating oneself
> running and hiding

Attack Other:
> "turning the tables"
> blaming the victim
> lashing out verbally or
   physically

Attack Self:
> self put-down
> masochism

Avoidance:
> denial
> abusing drugs and alcohol
> distraction through thrill-seeking

ADAPTED FROM NATHANSON, 1992

Several decades ago, the commonplace responses to shame were *attack self* and *withdrawal*. In *attack self*, the shamed individuals are self-punishing and unreasonably hard on themselves. In *withdrawal*, the shamed individuals hide because they are so overwhelmed by the shame.

These are normal responses to shame. However, they are harmful and need to be addressed. Conferences help people move beyond the compass of shame through acknowledgment and expression of shame and through subsequent reintegration. Because the conference affirms the intrinsic worth of the wrongdoer and condemns only the objectionable behavior, parents and offenders feel less threatened and more readily acknowledge responsibility.

Victims also experience shame. Victims may blame themselves for the offense, withdraw and hide their feelings, and sometimes distract themselves. Victims may lash out at others close to them who are not responsible for the offense. In providing an outlet for expressing feelings and moving beyond shame to resolution and reintegration, the conference is as important to victims as to offenders.

Restorative Justice

Restorative justice is a movement that developed in North America in the 1970s with the advent of victim-offender reconciliation programs. Although conferencing developed independently, it is now considered part of the restorative justice movement. We now use the term "restorative conferencing" to differentiate the process from the original New Zealand family group conferencing model.

Howard Zehr, in *Changing Lenses: A New Focus for Crime and Justice* (1990), described how restorative justice differs from our current justice system. Borrowing from Zehr, one sees how scripted conferencing differs from our current justice and school disciplinary systems:

1. Our current systems define an offense as a violation of the system, a crime against the state. In a conference an offense is defined as the harm that is done to a person or the community.

2. Our current systems focus on establishing blame or guilt. A conference focuses on solving problems and repairing harm.

3. Our current systems largely ignore the victim. The conference script supports the victims' rights and needs, providing an opportunity for victims to express feelings and help decide the outcome.

4. In our current systems the offender is passive. In a conference offenders are encouraged to take responsibility for their actions.

5. Our current systems define accountability as punishment. In a conference accountability means taking responsibility, apologizing and helping to repair the harm.

6. Our current response to crime and wrongdoing focuses on the offender's past behavior. A conference emphasizes the *harmful consequences* of the offender's behavior.

7. Under our current systems the stigma of crime is largely unremovable. The conference helps offenders overcome shame and stigma through appropriate actions.

8. In our current systems there is little encouragement for repentance. In a conference repentance is encouraged and forgiveness is possible.

9. Our current systems depend on professionals for justice. In a conference the facilitator stays in the background. The script encourages the direct involvement of those who have been affected.

10. Our current system is strictly rational. A conference encourages the free expression of emotion.

Why the Script?

The script reflects the human need to express and move beyond negative feelings, repair harm and resolve conflict. The script is easy to follow. It helps the facilitator stay anchored and focused, even in highly emotional situations. It is reliable, based on the experience of thousands of conferences. It is supported by sound psychological and sociological theory. It is a simple model that can be adapted easily to a broad range of offenses, conflicts and situations.

People may be tempted to change the script and make their own version. Some have made changes to the wording and organization of the script, often with undesirable results. Slight variations in wording can cause significant changes in responses.

The script presented here is supported by several research studies, which have consistently demonstrated high rates of participant satisfaction, perceptions of fairness and offender compliance with conference agreements (McCold & Wachtel, 1998; Moore & Forsythe, 1995; Umbreit & Fercello, 1998, 1999). Rarely has any new process been so thoroughly evaluated.

The argument for sticking to the script can be summarized by the popular maxim, "If it ain't broke, don't fix it." Facilitators take an unnecessary risk when they abandon or change the script.

CHAPTER 2

When to Run a Conference

Conferences for Offenders and Their Victims

The script in Chapter 1 was written for conferences dealing with criminal offenses and incidents of wrongdoing where offenders have admitted responsibility for the act and there is an identifiable victim. Although conferencing is now used in a variety of situations, including victimless crimes, this chapter focuses on clear-cut cases involving victims and offenders.

Conferencing can address victim-offender incidents in many settings—in schools, police departments, probation departments, courts, correctional facilities, workplaces, youth groups, summer camps and on college campuses. Any incident of wrongdoing—where harm has occurred and there is a need to repair that harm—is potentially appropriate for a conference. Within the justice system, the conference may be convened as a police or precourt diversion, as a means of deciding a sentence or fostering healing after adjudication, or as a reintegration ceremony when an offender is released from an institution to return home. In schools, the conference may serve as an alternative to detention, suspension and expulsion, or as a condition for the offending student returning to school after a suspension.

A single conference should be held for an incident, even when there are multiple offenders or multiple victims. Everyone involved with and affected by that incident should be invited. One offender may agree to participate, one offender may not, and another offender may be unable to attend. Similarly, some victims may participate and others may not. Nevertheless the conference may still be held, regardless of whether everyone attends.

For a conference to proceed, victims and offenders must voluntarily agree to participate, and offenders must admit to the offense. Where victims and offenders differ on facts or degrees of responsibility, facilitators should work to sort them out, making each party aware of the other's view prior to the conference. Victims may still want the conference to proceed, even if offenders have a conflicting perspective or are minimizing their responsibility.

If a conference is held when victims do not want to participate, facilitators should include the victims' perspective, preferably by inviting the victims' family and friends. Victims might write a letter, make an audio or video tape, or convey a message through the facilitator.

Some may question running a conference with offenders or victims who are physically or mentally disabled, mentally ill, emotionally disturbed, very young or very old. While such people may be unable to participate fully in the conference, they and their supporters can still benefit from the experience. Facilitators should enlist supporters who can help these individuals participate in the conference, understand what is happening and perhaps even interpret their behavior.

When offenders present a less than ideal attitude, facilitators should not avoid conferencing. A conference may help change that attitude. Some facilitators think they can predict which offenders will not participate appropriately or benefit from a conference, but that is unlikely. If facilitators are concerned, they should inform victims how the offenders are acting and let the victims decide if they want to proceed. Many victims simply want a chance to talk directly to offenders. Facilitators should not impose their fears. If no additional harm is likely to occur and victims are prepared for the encounter, a conference is a viable option. The decision to proceed belongs to the victims and offenders.

At the very least, conferences offer a chance for victims to express their feelings directly to offenders. Exchange of affect is usually beneficial. The process of human beings talking to each other will almost always be better than silent avoidance.

Who Should Facilitate the Conference?

A primary factor in deciding to run a conference is whether the facilitator has the experience needed for the particular case. This handbook, even if accompanied by the two-day Real Justice "Facilitating Restorative Conferences" training, will not prepare someone to facilitate a conference for violent offenses involving severe trauma for victims. However, if the facilitators have sufficient experience in dealing with serious crimes and their victims, they might appropriately facilitate such a conference.

Conferences may be facilitated by professionals as part of their jobs, specialists who are hired as full-time facilitators, screened and trained volunteers, or peers such as schoolmates, fellow inmates or coworkers. Facilitators should not run conferences for incidents that directly affected them or when they have played a counseling or support role with the offenders or victims.

Some people think that police officers or probation officers should not facilitate conferences as part of their professional role. Others believe that only volunteers are neutral enough to facilitate criminal justice conferences. These arbitrary limits on who should facilitate conferences are based on unsupported opinion and stereotyping. Research has consistently contradicted such constraints. A series of studies indicates that conference participants are satisfied with police officers running conferences (McCold & Wachtel, 1998; Moore & Forsythe, 1995; Umbreit & Fercello, 1998).

Conferences often transform the facilitator. Police, probation officers and educators who have become cynical are often surprised by the positive outcomes they see in a conference. Even when offenders later reoffend, the conference provides disheartened professionals with a hopeful glimpse of the potential of offenders and, if nothing else, allows them to see victims gain some healing and closure after a hurtful experience.

Time Frames

In most cases facilitators should move quickly, limiting the time between the incident and the conference to a couple of weeks. Unfortunately paperwork and procedures often interfere, so the time frame may be longer. If a conference is for a serious offense, victims may need more time to regain their equilibrium and prepare for meeting with the offenders. Grave offenses, like murder, may not result in a conference until years later.

When Not to Run a Conference

Before conferencing, facilitators should learn the details of the incident by speaking with everyone involved, including offenders, victims and their supporters. Certain details may not come to light until the facilitator has begun inviting people and preparing them for the conference. (Conference preparation will be discussed in detail in Chapter 3.)

Political considerations may influence whether to conference. In some jurisdictions, it may be easier and wiser for facilitators to start with lower-level offenses. Lower-level offenses are often simpler to facilitate, and the possible negative ramifications are smaller. At first, lesser offenses may be the only cases that are referred anyway. As facilitators gain experience and confidence in their abilities, others will gain confidence in them as well. Then the case flow and levels of offenses are likely to increase.

Facilitators should not accept cases that they do not have the experience to handle, such as incidents of severe trauma and sexual, physical or emotional abuse. Conferencing has been successful for these types of cases, but they may require significantly greater preparation, community resources and professional support, as well as relevant experience on the part of the facilitator. This manual is not focused on the most serious offenses, but on the other crime and wrongdoing, which comprise the bulk of offenses.

Time or space constraints may prevent facilitators from organizing a full conference. Some incidents may not seem serious enough to run a full conference. However, the level of seriousness is often not easy to discern. The way to find out is to talk to the victims, the ones most affected by the incident.

When a conference is not necessary or feasible but harm still needs to be repaired, the incident may still be resolved restoratively with an abbreviated conference or by using the questions and philosophy of the script in some other way. Chapter 6 will discuss these informal restorative practices.

Victim Needs

Most professionals attracted to conferencing and restorative justice are offender-focused. They want to help offenders turn their lives in a positive direction. However, when deciding whether to run a conference, they may overlook victim needs. For instance, many of the early police or court conferencing programs were limited to first-time offenders. Thus, if a victim's home was burglarized by a person with a prior offense, that victim was deprived of the opportunity to confront the offender, to have a say in the outcome and to enjoy the healing and closure that a conference might provide.

Victim needs are the priority in deciding whether to run a conference. According to research in victimology and restorative justice, victims may need:

> an opportunity to express their feelings
> acknowledgment from loved ones about what happened to them
> assurance that what happened was unfair and undeserved
> direct contact with offenders to hear the offender express shame and remorse, answer questions about the offense, and assure them that it won't happen again
> a sense of safety

A conference provides an ideal forum for victims to satisfy these needs.

CHAPTER 3

Conference Preparation

Careful preparation is crucial to facilitating successful conferences. Through preparation, facilitators can understand the incident, build rapport with participants and begin to envision how the conference may unfold. Use the Facilitator's Preparation Checklist at the end of this chapter as a reference.

A Note on Language

The terms "victim" and "offender" help facilitators keep track of participants and organize conferences. It would be unwieldy to keep saying "the person who was harmed" or "the person who caused the harm." However, facilitators should never use the terms "victim" and "offender" with conference participants because those terms can be stigmatizing. People should be referred to by their actual names whenever possible.

The terms "incident" and "offense" are used here interchangeably. In reality, for some cases and settings the term "offense" may seem extreme or legalistic. Conversely, for other cases and settings the term "incident" may seem minimizing or euphemistic. Facilitators should judge which term is appropriate.

Choosing a Time and Place

Facilitators should seek a conference room that is readily available or that they can reserve in advance. The room should be large enough for the expected number of participants, be private and free from interruptions and have access to restrooms. If possible, rooms should also have access to a copy machine for duplicating the conference agreement.

The conference location will depend on the jurisdiction but should be convenient, safe and easily accessible. Possibilities include the police station or community policing substation, the courthouse, a public or government building, a community center or school. To preserve the perceived fairness of the process, conferences are rarely held in the homes of conference participants. However, after consulting with the victim, offender and others, facilitators may occasionally deem this appropriate.

Scheduling the conference can sometimes be complicated, especially if there are multiple offenders or victims. Facilitators need a tentative time and date for the conference before contacting possible participants. Facilitators may shuttle between victims and offenders to find a mutually agreeable time. The victims' preference for a meeting time should be given the greatest weight.

Selecting and Inviting Participants

As a courtesy to victims, facilitators should first contact offenders and ensure their willingness to participate in a conference. This will save the victims any disappointment should the offenders decline. If there are multiple offenders, facilitators may begin inviting victims after one offender has agreed.

At a minimum, offenders should admit to the offense to be eligible for a conference, although some offenders may minimize or displace responsibility. Facilitators should address the offenders' need to take full responsibility during a preconference meeting.

When contacting people, facilitators explain the conference process and its benefits, answer questions, encourage and secure attendance at the conference, and build rapport and trust. It is *vital* for facilitators to speak with *all* participants before the conference, including victims, offenders, their supporters and others. Conferences where facilitators have not built rapport with all participants are much more likely to be problematic.

Facilitators must tailor their approach to offenders, victims and each set of supporters. Facilitators may create a brochure or information sheet that they can mail or give to people during their preconference meetings. The information for victims and their supporters may differ from that provided for offenders and their supporters.

People sometimes express concern that other participants will be disrespectful or offensive during the conference. In response, facilitators can explain that because participants usually feel conferencing is humane and trust the process, they tend to bring their "best selves" to the circle and participate in a constructive manner.

In many cases telephone contact is sufficient to explain the process and build rapport. Often facilitators will prefer to meet with victims and offenders in person. This is more time-consuming and not always feasible. However, when the offense is more serious or has complicated dynamics, an in-person meeting may raise participants' trust in the facilitator, improve the quality of the conference and more fully meet victims' needs. A personal visit may also ensure offenders take full responsibility for the incident, as well as increase the likelihood that victims, offenders and their families will participate. Personal visits are necessary when dealing with more serious offenses, and even with less serious offenses when victims are particularly upset.

When offenders are juveniles, facilitators may be legally required to contact their parents or guardian about the conference and perhaps gain their permission before speaking with the offender. However, if the offenders are of legal age, it may be considered a violation of their privacy to contact their parents without their permission, even if the offender is still in high school or attending a university or college.

Determining who to invite as supporters is an important part of conference preparation. Victims and offenders may nominate anyone they choose. Facilitators may also invite individuals who do not clearly fall into the category of victim, victim supporter or offender supporter, but who have been directly affected by the incident in some way—perhaps someone who witnessed the incident or an investigating police officer. Sometimes victims and offenders make the initial contact with their nominated supporters to tell them about the conference and to let them know the facilitator will call.

Young children may participate in conferences, if they can speak and basically understand what is going on. Even if the conference deals with severe offenses, children can still participate because they have been harmed by those offenses and need healing as much as adults. Script questions may need to be adapted slightly to a child's level of understanding.

Offenders and victims should not have legal counsel at the conference. The facilitator should advise any attorneys who want to be involved that a conference is not a legal proceeding and that they may attend only as a supporter, like other supporters who are connected to the victim or offender, or as a silent observer sitting outside the circle.

Facilitators should know local laws regarding whether disclosures made in a conference are admissible in court and advise offenders accordingly. In practice, however, the conference almost always settles the matter without further legal proceedings.

When facilitators receive a case, they must learn what will happen if the case does not result in a conference, if no agreement is reached, or if the offender fails to satisfy the agreement. If there is no protocol, facilitators need to discuss the matter with those who have the authority to decide.

It is difficult to say exactly how many people should attend a conference. It depends on the offenders' and victims' support networks, the number of offenders and victims and the nature of the offense. Most conferences have 8 to 15 participants and run 30 to 90 minutes. Larger conferences may run as long as 2 to 4 hours. Generally the more people in a conference, the longer it will take.

Usually, the more people in a conference, the better, because of the wider variety of personalities. Smaller groups may be dominated by one or two individuals who may or may not be positive influences. In larger groups there is an averaging or normalizing effect, with the more extreme personalities balanced by others in the circle. In fact, facilitators running larger conferences are more likely to find the balance maintained by the participants themselves.

Inviting as many as possible to a conference also offers the opportunity to develop "communities of care" for the victim and offender. Often the victim's community and the offender's community become one community. Because an incident of wrongdoing brings relationships into critical focus, the conference can be a beginning point for establishing and building relationships. The conference allows the building of social bonds, which are needed to sustain healthy family and community relationships.

Facilitators with a mediation background often worry about power imbalances, but the conference framework deals with those issues naturally. With supporters for both offenders and victims, the power balance between individuals is evened out. There is no need to have the same number of participants for each "side"— offender and victim. However, if facilitators know that one group is particularly large, they can encourage the other group to bring more supporters.

Inviting official community representatives or others who do not have a direct emotional connection with the incident may be a problem. They sometimes preach or moralize, dampening the affective exchange. If community representatives are included, they should be coached to speak personally about how the incident made them feel.

Contacting Offenders and Young Offenders' Parents

When contacting offenders, facilitators should introduce themselves and explain the purpose of the conference. For example:

"Hi, my name is (facilitator's name). I'm with (facilitator's agency), and I'm working on setting up a conference dealing with (brief description of offense). I'd like to offer you an opportunity to attend a conference instead of (referring the matter to court/ handling the matter through school disciplinary procedures/ handling the matter in another way). The conference will help us learn how people have been affected by what you did and how to repair the harm that has resulted. We are not going to decide whether you are good or bad. We just want to discuss how your inappropriate behavior affected other people and how to repair the harm."

Facilitators should explain the conference process, who will be present and what the offender can expect to be asked at the conference. If the offender is not of legal age, facilitators may need to contact the offender's parents or guardian before speaking with the offender.

For offenders and the parents of young offenders, facilitators should describe the advantages of the conference process from their perspective. These include: the opportunity for offenders to understand the consequences of their behavior, learning how the incident has affected their family and friends, helping develop and implement a plan to repair the harm and disapproving of the offenders' behavior while affirming their worth as members of the community. The conference is an alternative to more punitive disciplinary processes or a way to avoid formal criminal charges. However, conferences are not the "easier" option some might assume.

With young offenders, facilitators may speak with offenders and their parents together, but it is important to speak with each individually as well. Facilitators need to establish individual rapport with offenders and work to ensure that offenders begin the conference by accepting responsibility for what they did, without rationalizing, minimizing or making excuses.

Accepting responsibility and owning the behavior go beyond a simple admission. In conferences where offenders do not own their behavior, other participants usually become morally indignant, decreasing the chances of successfully reaching a conference agreement. Preparing the offender can avoid this pitfall.

Facilitators prepare offenders during their preconference meetings by having them say what happened in their own words. Facilitators should speak to offenders in a positive tone and listen to the offenders tell their stories. Some offenders readily take responsibility for their behavior, saying how sorry they are and that they know it was wrong. In this case, facilitators should offer encouragement and tell offenders that if they speak so humbly and honestly during the conference, the process will probably go very well.

Other offenders make excuses and blame others. When facilitators detect this, they should stop the offender and say something like:

"I want to make sure that this conference goes well for you. I hear you describing what happened and though you've admitted that you did it, you seem to be blaming others, which will just make everyone angry with you. If you have some reasons why things happened the way they did, save them for later in the conference. Just start out really honest and humble, admitting what you did without any explanations. Then the conference will go better. Do you know what I mean? Why don't you try it again, this time just saying what you did and admitting it was wrong."

Facilitators should listen again and give compliments if the offender seems to be owning the behavior. Facilitators may even tell offenders that people will respond better if they say it the same way during the conference. As a closing statement, facilitators can ask offenders to think about how people have been affected by their actions.

This preparation helps offenders—especially young people who may not have the communication skills to humbly express remorse—start on the right foot in the conference. If an offender's attitude is a deceptive ploy, that will usually become obvious as the conference continues. In most cases, however, offenders are favorably affected by the conference atmosphere, and their honesty and positive attitude is reinforced, even if they were not totally sincere at the outset.

During preconference meetings, offenders and their parents may rationalize or minimize the offense by blaming other people and situations. Blaming others for the incident often reflects an underlying feeling of shame. For example, sometimes offenders or parents of offenders who assaulted someone may claim that the victim "egged them on" or was "asking for it."

While there are often other factors that contributed to the offense, facilitators should say that what the offenders did was unacceptable and that they need to take responsibility for their part in what happened. Asking questions in the preconference meeting such as "If you had it to do over again, what would you do differently?" or "How could you have responded differently?" can help offenders realize that they could have chosen less harmful responses.

Parents may have much to say about the incident and the offender, as well as how they have been personally affected. Facilitators should listen attentively and compassionately, allowing ventilation of feelings and expression of opinions.

Parents of offenders may express anger with the offender. Degrading statements about offenders and their individual worth, such as name-calling and other stigmatizing characterizations, can be dangerous. For example, "John is such a troublemaker" or "Carrie is just like her mother." Facilitators should acknowledge the anger and help the parents explore it, by saying, for example, "You seem very angry about what happened. Can you tell me more about that?" There are usually underlying feelings of hurt, disappointment, frustration and shame. Encourage them to express those feelings, rather than characterize the offender as good or bad.

Offenders nominate supporters to be at the conference. The ideal offender supporter is someone whom the offender cares about, who can strongly disapprove of the inappropriate behavior while affirming the offender's positive qualities and worth. When exploring who to invite as offender supporters, facilitators should help the offender think creatively about who is important to them and who can be supportive to them at the conference—including parents, brothers, sisters, extended family, friends, peers, spouses, counselors, coaches, priests, rabbis, neighbors and others. Facilitators can ask offenders, "Who in your life really cares about you?" then ask about people in the different areas of the offenders' life, such as family, school, work, church, clubs and sports. Some offenders have little family support, but might have a social worker, counselor or even probation officer they like and want to have with them at the conference.

Sometimes offenders do not want supporters, usually because they are ashamed for others to know what they did. However, the conference process depends on the inclusion of the offender's "community of care," because offenders are more likely to hear the effects of their actions, acknowledge their shame and express remorse when people that they care about are present. The person the offender seems least comfortable inviting may be the one the facilitator should persuade the offender to invite. Sometimes, particularly in the case of juvenile offenses, parents have every right to attend, and perhaps even extended family members, without the permission of the youth.

When offenders do not readily nominate supporters, facilitators may ask people who know the offender who they think could be a supporter. Even when offenders have no family and friends nearby, there are often people in the community who have had contact with the offenders who can offer support. Conferences help to create or strengthen positive bonds between offenders and people in their community.

If offenders insist that they do not want any supporters at the conference, facilitators should say that part of the offenders' positive participation in the conference includes having supporters there, because they offer a special perspective on the offender and can contribute to the conference process and resolution. Facilitators must make it difficult for the offender to refuse supporters.

Before ending the preconference meeting, facilitators should address any remaining questions. If they have a tentative time and date for the conference, they should make sure it is acceptable to the offender, but say it may have to be shifted to suit the victim. Facilitators should ask the offender for alternative times. Facilitators should ensure that offenders and their parents know how to find the conference site, and possibly offer transportation or provide directions. Lastly facilitators should leave their business card or their written phone number in case offenders or parents need to contact them.

Contacting Victims

When contacting victims, facilitators begin by introducing themselves and explaining the purpose of the conference. For example:

"Hi, my name is (facilitator's name). I'm with (facilitator's agency), and I'm working on setting up a conference dealing with (brief description of offense), in which you were unfortunately harmed. I am organizing a conference to deal with the incident because it can provide you with an opportunity to meet (offender's name), tell (offender's name) how you were affected, ask questions and have direct involvement in deciding what happens. I'd like to tell you about the conference and answer your questions, so you can decide if you would like to participate. The conference is an alternative to (referring the matter to court/handling the matter through school disciplinary procedures/handling the matter in another way), and most people find it a more satisfying way to repair the harm that has resulted. (Offender's name) has admitted committing the offense and has agreed to participate in the conference. While I can't guarantee what the outcome of the conference will be, I can tell you that it usually goes very well."

Facilitators should explain the conference process, who will be present, what will be asked and what victims can reasonably expect. Facilitators should describe to victims the potential benefits of the conference process, which include: telling the offender how they were affected, holding the offender accountable and having a say in how to repair the harm, possibly receiving an apology and restitution and asking the offender questions about the offense.

The facilitator's primary job in preconference meetings with victims is to listen to them relate their feelings and how they were affected by the incident. Facilitators should allow victims as much time as they need to do this. Even if victims decline participation or if the conference is not held for some other reason, victims may still appreciate that someone took the time to listen to them—a significant contribution to the healing process.

Facilitators must not pressure victims to participate in a conference. Facilitators can tell victims the advantages of the conference and how other victims have responded to the process. Facilitators should also tell victims if the offenders express a different view about what happened or if offenders seem particularly lacking in remorse. While facilitators should not "sell" the victim on the conference, they can express their enthusiasm for the value of conferencing. If victims decline participation, facilitators should thank them for their consideration.

Victims may nominate anyone they like to support them at the conference. Victims are generally more forthcoming than offenders in nominating supporters, although not always. When victims hesitate to nominate supporters, facilitators should stress that they may feel more comfortable at the conference if they have people to support them. Facilitators should also stress that the victims' family and friends should be at the conference because they have also been affected by the harm done to someone close to them.

Facilitators should check with the victim whether the time, date and location of the conference are convenient. Before ending the meeting, facilitators should answer any remaining questions, provide directions to the conference site if needed, possibly offer transportation and leave their business card or written phone number in case the victim has additional questions.

Contacting Offender and Victim Supporters

Facilitators should speak with *all* supporters before the conference. Building rapport with supporters increases the chances of a successful conference because they will be more likely to work with the facilitator to see that the process goes well.

When contacting offender and victim supporters, facilitators must introduce themselves and explain the conference process, how the conference will benefit the victim, offender and themselves and why their participation will be helpful. For example:

"Hi, my name is (facilitator's name). I'm with (facilitator's agency), and I'm working on setting up a conference dealing with (brief description of offense). (Offender's name or victim's name) has asked for you to be at the conference to support them. The conference will help us learn how people have been affected by what happened and how to repair the harm that has resulted. Your presence would benefit the process, and I know (offender's name or victim's name) would like you to attend."

Sometimes supporters know little or nothing about the incident, so facilitators may tell them more about what happened. It may help if victims or offenders contact their nominated supporters to explain the conference and let them know the facilitator will be calling.

Offender and victim supporters may simply see themselves as providing support. Often, however, they have been directly affected by the incident and need to express their feelings—particularly close friends and relatives of victims of more serious crimes. Facilitators should give supporters the same respect and attention as victims, listening and allowing them to discuss their thoughts and feelings.

Like parents of offenders, offender supporters may feel angry and ashamed about what the offender did. Facilitators should reframe degrading or stigmatizing statements and focus on the underlying feelings of shame, disappointment and hurt.

Before ending the meeting, facilitators should answer any remaining questions, ensure supporters know the conference time, date and location, provide directions to the site if needed, possibly offer transportation and leave their business card or written phone number in case the supporters have additional questions.

The Seating Plan

Facilitators should develop a conference seating plan. (See Figure 3 and Figure 4.) In the conference, participants should be seated close together in a circle or oval shape, with no tables or other obstructions in the middle. Tables can inhibit emotional expression because they obscure body language and can be used as protective barriers by participants. The circle also symbolizes community or "coming together."

CONFERENCE SEATING GUIDE
Figure 3

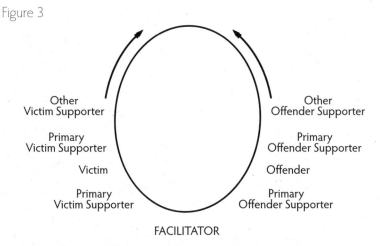

Offenders and their supporters should sit in the circle on one side of the facilitator, and victims and their supporters should sit in the circle on the other side of the facilitator. The offender group generally sits on the right and the victim group on the left. This is arbitrary, but facilitators should adopt one approach—offender right/victim left *or* offender left/victim right—and stick with it over time to help them manage their conferences more smoothly.

Offenders and victims should sit next to their closest supporters and near, but not necessarily next to, the facilitator. For young offenders, their closest supporters are usually parents or guardians, who can sit to either side. If there are multiple offenders, each should sit between their closest supporters.

Other victim supporters and offender supporters should sit on their respective sides of the circle, with both groups' seating progressing away from the facilitator toward the point in the circle opposite the facilitator.

CONFERENCE SEATING PLANNER
Figure 4

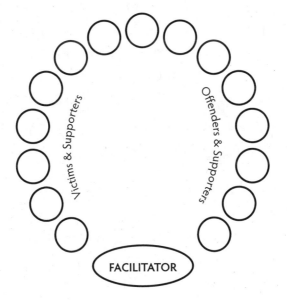

Victims & Supporters

Offenders & Supporters

FACILITATOR

Participants who are not explicitly a victim or offender supporter, such as an investigating police officer, can be seated between the two groups, opposite the facilitator. If facilitators feel that a particular participant may be disruptive or troublesome in the conference, they may choose to seat that participant nearest to them to make it more uncomfortable for that person to be disruptive.

Large Conferences

On the rare occasion when a conference is particularly large, perhaps 30 or more people, facilitators should arrange participants in rows of chairs, with victims and their supporters facing offenders and their supporters and the facilitator seated between the two groups, as in Figure 5 below.

LARGE CONFERENCE DIAGRAM
Figure 5

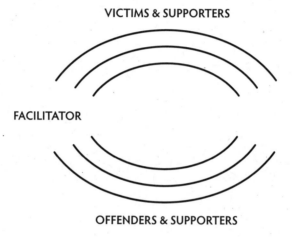

VICTIMS & SUPPORTERS

FACILITATOR

OFFENDERS & SUPPORTERS

Because of the time and number of people involved in large conferences, facilitators will need help seating people, answering questions, taking care of unexpected problems and guiding people to restrooms and refreshments—which should be available throughout the conference. The assistant or co-facilitator may chat with people when they have refreshments and encourage them to return to the conference because some may be discouraged by the duration. A large pad of paper, easel and marker are useful for constructing the conference agreement.

Additional Preparation

Facilitators should envision how the conference may unfold. This becomes easier as facilitators gain experience and understanding of the dynamics of conferences. Their trust in the process will grow as well.

Each conference is unique, but patterns emerge that help facilitators organize and prepare. For instance, if the offender readily takes responsibility in the start of the conference, victims and others are less likely to express moral indignation. Or if the offender's parents are harsh with the offender, other participants may say something positive or supportive about the offender.

Each facilitator will develop a way of organizing conference preparation materials. Facilitators should record the phone numbers and addresses of conference participants and other relevant contacts. They may also keep notes on their discussions with conference participants and others to review during conference preparation or for later reference.

Facilitators should be familiar with the conference script and read through it to determine the order that participants will speak, noting the order on the script or seating plan. Labels with participants' names can be placed on the seats before participants arrive. Facilitators should ensure that the conference room is reserved and that all participants were told the correct time, date and location of the conference. Facilitators may put a sign on the door saying, "Do Not Disturb: Conference In Progress." Also, facilitators will provide tissues, which signify to participants that emotional expression is acceptable, and refreshments for the informal period after the conference.

If facilitators are concerned about handling a particular situation, they should seek advice from a colleague who has been trained in facilitating Real Justice conferences. The IIRP provides direct support for facilitators, via telephone and email.

Facilitator's Preparation Checklist

☐ Do you have a clear understanding of the incident?

☐ Is a conference needed?

☐ Has the offender admitted responsibility?

☐ Have you invited all necessary participants?

☐ Have you spoken or met with all participants and secured their attendance?

☐ Do participants understand the conference process and its purpose?

☐ Do participants know how to contact you?

☐ Have you reserved a suitable room?

☐ Do participants know the time, date and location, and how to get there?

☐ Do participants have transportation?

☐ Have you developed a seating plan?

☐ Are you familiar with the conference facilitator's script?

☐ Have you thought about how the conference may unfold?

☐ Do you need assistance, a co-facilitator or an observer to give you feedback?

☐ Do you know what may happen if the conference does not reach an agreement or the offender fails to satisfy the agreement?

☐ Do you have the following items for the conference?
    ☐ a copy of the conference facilitator's script
    ☐ agreement forms and other required forms
    ☐ the conference seating plan
    ☐ participant seating labels
    ☐ a "Do Not Disturb" sign
    ☐ a box of tissues
    ☐ refreshments

Running the Conference

Before the Conference

Before participants arrive, facilitators set up the conference room, arranging chairs according to the seating plan and taking into account any last-minute changes. There should be no tables or other physical obstructions within the circle of chairs. Labels with participants' names may be placed on the chairs to help the seating process. Facilitators should bring their conference script (see chapter 1 or download from www.realjustice.org/pdf/script.pdf), agreement forms, seating plan, a box of tissues and refreshments for the informal period after the conference.

The room should be free from noise and visual distractions, such as a window looking out onto a busy street. If there is a phone or intercom in the room, the ringer should be turned off. A "Do Not Disturb: Conference In Progress" sign may be placed on doors accessing the room. Facilitators should locate the nearest restrooms so they can direct participants to them. Facilitators also need access to a photocopier to duplicate the conference agreement after it is signed.

If possible, there should be separate waiting areas for victims and their supporters and offenders and their supporters to avoid the mutual discomfort of facing each other in silence before the conference convenes. When participants arrive, the facilitator should meet them and direct them to a waiting area. Facilitators should be courteous and respectful, and maintain the formality and seriousness of the occasion. An assistant may help facilitators greet and direct participants. Facilitators should keep track of who has arrived.

Sometimes facilitators meet with each group separately, just before the conference, to review the conference process, address last-minute questions or concerns and explain the seating arrangements. This is optional.

If an offender, victim or key supporter is late, facilitators should wait a reasonable amount of time, perhaps telephoning the individual. If there is one offender or one victim, and either does not show up to the conference, the conference should be rescheduled if possible. If it seems that a full conference will not occur, a modified conference may address the needs of the people who have been assembled.

If a peripheral supporter has not arrived, facilitators may wait a short time and then begin the conference. It is not a good idea to admit participants once the conference has begun. Their perspective will differ from other participants who have experienced the conference from the beginning. Facilitators may allow latecomers to observe the conference from outside the circle or participate in some limited way, depending on when they arrive.

If victims or offenders bring unexpected supporters, facilitators usually allow them to participate. However, facilitators should speak with them about the conference process and purpose and tell them what they will be asked in the conference. If it appears the unexpected supporters are indignant and may sabotage the conference process—on purpose or inadvertently—facilitators should speak with them further. Facilitators should explain that much preparation has gone into the conference, that all who came to the conference took time from their days and are invested in the conference going well, and that they are welcome to participate in a respectful and constructive manner.

If an offender comes without supporters, facilitators may choose not to conference, reschedule or confer with victims and others about whether to proceed.

If a participant is obviously intoxicated, they should not participate, out of respect for the rest of the participants. If facilitators merely suspect that a participant is intoxicated, they should rely on their judgment to determine if that person will be disruptive, monitor them during the conference and ask them to leave later if they behave inappropriately.

To begin the conference, facilitators bring one group into the conference room at a time, preferably the victim's group first. When everyone is seated, the facilitator begins the conference. There should generally be no interruptions after starting.

Facilitators should have a clipboard or folder with the seating plan, the conference script, blank paper for developing the conference agreement and agreement forms or other forms to be completed.

Throughout the conference, facilitators should be calm, take their time, speak evenly and allow silence between speakers and questions. They should always be respectful, especially when responding to a challenge. Facilitators should never express personal opinions about the incident or make suggestions. However, as guardians of the conference process, they must be ready to assert themselves with participants who stray from the conference focus or otherwise disrupt the process.

Below is a description of the conference script and its phases. Sections from the script are indented and in a different typeface.

The Preamble

Facilitators begin the conference by welcoming everyone, introducing themselves and then participants, saying their names and stating their relationships to the offender or victim.

1. PREAMBLE

"Welcome. As you know, my name is (your name) **and I will be facilitating this conference."**

Now introduce each conference participant and state his/her relationship to the offender/s or victim/s.

For the introductions, facilitators will generally state each person's first and last names. Facilitators should never use the terms "offender" and "victim" to describe individuals during the conference. Depending on the setting, the age and status of the participants, facilitators may also include prefixes or titles instead of or in addition to first names, such as "Mr./Mrs./Ms./Dr.," "officer" or "principal." For example: "This is Chris Rogers, whose behavior we are here to discuss today. This is Steve Rogers, Chris's father, and Laura Rogers, Chris's sister. This is Bob Reading, Chris's basketball coach. This is Officer Johnson, who conducted the initial investigation and made the arrest. This is Mary Huang, whose car tires were slashed by Chris, and this is Mary's husband, John Huang. And lastly, this is Cindy Smith, Mary's friend."

How facilitators introduce participants frames their roles in the conference. It may help to reiterate each participant's relationship to the victim or offender the first couple of times they are addressed. For example, "Let's speak now with Bob Reading, Chris's basketball coach. Mr. Reading, what did you think when you heard about the incident?"

After introducing participants, facilitators should thank everyone for attending and set the conference focus—to explore how people have been affected by the incident and how to repair the harm that has resulted. The description of the incident should be brief.

> **"Thank you all for attending. I know that this is difficult for all of you, but your presence will help us deal with the matter that has brought us together. This is an opportunity for all of you to be involved in repairing the harm that has been done."**

> **"This conference will focus on an incident that happened** (state the date, place and nature of offense without elaborating)**. It is important to understand that we will focus on what** (offender name/s) **did and how that unacceptable behavior has affected others. We are not here to decide whether** (offender name/s) is/are **good or bad. We want to explore in what way people have been affected and hopefully work toward repairing the harm that has resulted. Does everyone understand this?"**

The conference focus tells participants what will happen without prescribing the outcome. During the conference, facilitators can restate the focus when participants are off track. If a participant calls the offender names or uses stigmatizing or degrading language, the facilitator can restate a phrase from the preamble: "We are not here to decide whether (offender name/s) is good or bad. We want to explore in what way people have been affected..." Repeating portions of the preamble reminds people of the intended tone and purpose of the conference and allows the facilitator to avoid direct confrontation with participants. They tend to honor this redirection because they already have a positive rapport with the facilitator.

After setting the focus, facilitators should remind offenders, as well as other participants, that they have the right to leave the conference. Offenders must acknowledge that if they do leave, the incident may be handled in a different way, perhaps through a formal judicial or disciplinary process.

> "(Offender name/s) **has**/have **admitted his**/her/their **part in the incident."**

> Say to offender/s: **"I must tell you that you do not have to participate in this conference and are free to leave at any time, as is anyone else. If you do leave, the matter may be referred to court**/handled by the school disciplinary policy/handled in another way."

> "This matter, however, may be finalized if you participate in a positive manner and comply with the conference agreement."

> Say to offender/s: **"Do you understand?"**

This portion of the script was initially added to safeguard the offenders' right to due process in the criminal justice system. Facilitators might also ask the parents of young offenders to acknowledge their children's rights as well. The phrase "as is anyone else" was added later to clarify that all participants have the right to leave at any time.

In addition to admitting responsibility for the offense, offenders are expected to participate in the conference in a positive manner and carry out commitments they make in the conference.

Speaking With Offenders

Offenders are asked to speak before the victims or any other participants in the conference. A consensus has developed among experienced conference facilitators that having offenders speak first is beneficial to victims and the whole conference process. This consensus is supported by studies showing high rates of victim satisfaction with the conferencing process.

Many victims have said that they would prefer for offenders to go first, rather than be put "on the spot." More often than not, the offenders take responsibility for the offense in a way that reduces victims' anger, anxiety and moral indignation—thereby saving victims a great deal of unpleasantness.

Offenders speaking first eliminates false preconceptions among participants about the offender's attitude, allowing a more informed and realistic exchange. Defensiveness from the offenders' parents and other supporters can be avoided if they hear what the offenders have done, in the offenders' own words.

If offenders refuse responsibility, the facilitator should address this immediately. The facilitator and the participants may decide not to proceed with the conference. If the conference does proceed, participants can take the offender's attitude into account.

Clarifying the offender's attitude up front allows the conference to move toward more satisfying and useful activities—exploring how people were affected and repairing harm. Also, if victims and other participants were to start the conference by verbally attacking an offender who is already predisposed to take appropriate responsibility, the process would be unnecessarily complicated.

2. OFFENDER/S
"We'll start with (one of offenders' names)**."**

If there is more than one offender, have each respond to all of the following questions.

> **"What happened?"**
> **"What were you thinking about at the time?"**
> **"What have you thought about since the incident?"**

> ﹥ **"Who do you think has been affected by your actions?"**
> ﹥ **"How have they been affected?"**

When there are multiple offenders, facilitators may ask each offender every question, one offender at a time. Depending on their experience and comfort level, facilitators may alternate between offenders. This gives all offenders equal opportunity to take responsibility early in the conference. It can build a fuller picture of what happened and help address any discrepancies between the offenders' stories.

Some offenders will give short answers, leave out details or find it difficult to speak at all. Facilitators should allow extended silence, so offenders can think about what to say and know that the facilitator is not just going to move on if they do not answer. Silence is a powerful tool for overcoming an offender's passive resistance. In a respectful way, silence makes it uncomfortable for the offender to stay aloof from the conference. It is OK for offenders to feel uncomfortable. After a period of silence, the facilitator may restate the question.

Follow-up or clarifying questions may be necessary, particularly when offenders are describing what happened. Some follow-up questions might be: "Could you tell us more about that?" "What did you do after that?" "What happened next?"

Facilitators should not worry about small discrepancies in facts, nor should they rigorously challenge offenders on their statements. Offenders need not fill in every single detail of the offense, the events leading up to it and afterward. However, they should clearly state their roles and responsibility, without making excuses or blaming others.

Despite follow-up questions and extended silences, some offenders may say little or take little responsibility. Other participants may spontaneously confront or ask questions of the offender.

Facilitators should allow this as long as the discussion stays on track. If the discussion moves off focus, the facilitator should restate the language from the preamble that describes the conference focus, ask the offender another question, or if the offender has already answered all five questions, move on.

If offenders deny the offense, the facilitator may say that a condition for holding the conference was that the offenders admitted their part in the incident, but now they are denying it. Facilitators can remind offenders about what they said during a preconference meeting. If offenders continue to deny responsibility, the facilitator may stop the conference or allow participants to discuss whether they want to continue.

If participants, especially victims, want to continue despite the offenders' denial, and the offender chooses to stay, the facilitator can allow it. Offenders may reverse their denial, or participants may "agree to disagree," figuring that despite the differences in people's versions of the facts, something can still be gained from the conference. However, if an impasse is reached that cannot be resolved after a reasonable amount of discussion, the conference should be ended. The decision to end a conference is rare and should be exercised with caution.

Sometimes other conference participants will shift the blame for the offense. Parents may blame the school for not properly supervising their child. The offender and victim groups may unite and blame the police or the school for mishandling the situation. While these situations are rare, if facilitators have adequate rapport with participants, they can be dealt with by refocusing the discussion. If participants continue to shift blame, the facilitator may allow a limited time to address the issue, particularly if the "accused" party is present. If participants do not move beyond this stance, even after lengthy discussion, the facilitator should end the conference.

Occasionally offenders in conferences may smile or otherwise act inappropriately. While this is probably due to anxiety or a lack of social skills, other participants may see the behavior as contemptuous or defiant. If necessary, facilitators can intervene by asking offenders about their behavior, whether they realized what they were doing, or by asking their parents or other offender supporters to interpret the behavior.

Speaking With Victims

Having victims and their supporters speak before the offender supporters further confronts the offender group with the reality of what the offender has done, helping to avoid potential defensiveness and rationalization of the offenders' behavior. When offenders are done speaking, facilitators should cue victims to speak. Facilitators can precede their questions with a statement such as "Now let's find out from (name of victim) how he/she has been affected."

3. <u>VICTIM/S</u>

If there is more than one victim, have each respond to all of the following questions.

> **"What was your reaction at the time of the incident?"**
> **"How do you feel about what happened?"**
> **"What has been the hardest thing for you?"**
> **"How did your family and friends react when they heard about the incident?"**

Facilitators should again allow plenty of time and silence for victims to think and respond to questions. For their first few conferences, facilitators should simply ask all four questions in the suggested order. With some experience, facilitators may decide to skip a question if it has already been fully answered. This should be an exception, rather than a rule. A differently phrased question—even if it has already been answered—can elicit a different response or an elaboration.

Victims are generally forthcoming in describing their thoughts and feelings. Their responses will depend on what the offenders said and how they perceive the offenders. If the offenders show remorse and appropriate responsibility, victims may be more understanding and sometimes are remarkably generous.

If the offenders have failed to take responsibility or show remorse, victims may understandably display moral indignation. Facilitators should allow victims to vent their feelings. On the rare occasion when a victim verbally abuses the offender, the facilitator may respectfully remind the victim that "we are here to learn how everyone has been affected, but please let's not call each other names."

If a victim has difficulty speaking, facilitators can allow the victim time to respond or regain composure, or possibly move on to others and get back to that victim later.

Victims may directly ask the offender questions, which the facilitator should allow. Victims often want to know why offenders committed the offense and why the offenders chose them to victimize, and want to be assured it will not happen again. If the offender was not forthcoming or remorseful, victims may have many challenging questions.

Speaking With Victim Supporters

When it seems that victims have fully responded to the questions and are finished speaking, facilitators should begin questioning the victim supporters. The victim's closest supporters should be asked to speak first.

4. <u>VICTIM SUPPORTERS</u>

Have each respond to all of the following questions.

> **"What did you think when you heard about the incident?"**

> **"How do you feel about what happened?"**
> **"What has been the hardest thing for you?"**
> **"What do you think are the main issues?"**

Facilitators should allow plenty of time for participants to respond to questions. As with victims, victim supporters' responses will depend on the offenders' apparent attitude, acceptance of responsibility and level of remorse.

Some participants may interact spontaneously. Facilitators can allow this but should ensure that each participant has the opportunity to fully answer all questions. Facilitators can let the discussion go for a time and then refocus by asking the next question from the script. When the victim supporters have spoken, facilitators should move to the offender supporters.

Speaking With Offender Supporters

The first offender supporter the facilitator questions should have the strongest attachment to the offender and be most likely to exhibit the strongest emotional response. If the offender is a youth, this is usually the offender's mother. The facilitator should say, "This has been difficult for you, hasn't it? Would you like to tell us about it?" before asking the remaining four questions from the script.

5. <u>OFFENDER SUPPORTERS</u>

To parent/caregiver ask: **"This has been difficult for you, hasn't it? Would you like to tell us about it?"**

Have each respond to all of the following questions.

> **"What did you think when you heard about the incident?"**
> **"How do you feel about what happened?"**
> **"What has been the hardest thing for you?"**

> **"What do you think are the main issues?"**

Continuing with the next closest in relation to the offender, other offender supporters should then be asked these last four questions. Sometimes participants interact spontaneously, and facilitators should ensure that each participant has an opportunity to speak. Usually participants will wait until they are directly addressed.

Parents of offenders often express intense feelings of distress and shame. Facilitators should allow silences and not rush to the next part of the script. Offender supporters are primary triggers of the offenders' shame and remorse about their wrongdoing.

Offender supporters sometimes defend or rationalize what the offender did. This can undermine the conference and diminish the significance of the harm the offender caused. Facilitators may refocus the conference by re-stating part of the preamble.

More often, offender supporters will try to show remorse by taking a tough stance against the offender. If this manifests itself as stigmatizing or degrading statements toward the offender, the facilitator may intervene. Other participants, including victims and their supporters, may refocus the discussion before the facilitator needs to act.

Offender supporters sometimes say they were surprised or shocked or disappointed by what the offender did. This is an opportunity to help offender supporters make the distinction between the offense and the offender. The facilitator can ask them why they felt that way. They may make statements such as "because he is normally a good kid" or "because she usually doesn't act that way." These statements show that while the offense was inappropriate, the offender does have good qualities.

The Agreement Phase

When all participants have spoken, participants may continue to interact. They will often turn to issues of reparation and apology on their own. To help the process of reparation, the facilitator should—at some appropriate point—ask the next question from the script.

6. OFFENDER/S
Ask the offender/s: **"Is there anything you want to say at this time?"**

Sometimes offenders may have nothing to say. Often, however, they will apologize to victims, their family and others in the conference. Next the facilitator should ask the victims what they would like from the conference, involving offenders and the rest of the conference participants in the process of creating a conference agreement.

7. REACHING AN AGREEMENT
Ask the victim/s: **"What would you like from today's conference?"**

Ask the offender/s to respond.

At this point, the participants discuss what should be in the final agreement. Solicit comments from participants.

It is important that you ask the offender/s to respond to each suggestion before the group moves to the next suggestion, asking **"What do you think about that?"** Then determine that the offender/s agree/s before moving on. Allow for negotiation.

As the agreement develops, clarify each item and make the written document as specific as possible, including details, deadlines and follow-up arrangements.

As you sense that the agreement discussion is drawing to a close, say to the participants:

"Before I prepare the written agreement, I'd like to make sure that I have accurately recorded what has been decided."

Read the items in the agreement aloud and look to the participants for acknowledgment. Make any necessary corrections.

The agreement phase is the least structured part of the conference. Participants freely discuss their ideas for how to repair the harm. The facilitator clarifies and records items accurately and in detail, checks with the victim, offender and other participants that they are OK with each item, and monitors discussions to ensure participants stay focused. Facilitators should encourage a variety of ideas and allow plenty of time for discussion. If discussion is limited, facilitators may canvas participants for their suggestions and comments.

Most conferences lead to a mutually acceptable agreement. The ultimate decision to include an item in the agreement is the offender's and the victim's. Typically the conference agreement is written during the conference and signed by victims, offenders and parents of young offenders, or perhaps by all participants, shortly after the conference. On rare occasions conferences may simply result in a spoken understanding among participants. Conference outcomes vary greatly, depending on the circumstances of the offense, the needs of the participants and the offenders' attitude in the conference.

Facilitators should not impose their opinions or suggestions on the conference agreement. For instance, they should not recommend that every offender complete community service. If participants decide that community service is appropriate, facilitators may then provide information on community service options.

On rare occasions when facilitators feel that items in the agreement are unreasonable, harsh or that there is an excessive number of conditions, facilitators may "reality test" by tactfully asking if participants have similar concerns. If everyone, including the offender, is comfortable with the agreement as it stands, then the facilitator should defer.

If the agreement includes personal service by offenders for the victim, facilitators should make sure that victims are comfortable with this. Victims may ask a conference participant to accompany the offender when they do the task.

Facilitators should never imply or suggest that offenders apologize, nor should they encourage victims to forgive offenders. Genuine apology and forgiveness is voluntarily and spontaneously offered, not coerced.

Sometimes all victims want is a spoken or written apology. Facilitators should *never* insist that offenders do more than the participants have agreed to, even if they think the offender is getting off easy. Symbolic reparation—apology, forgiveness, reintegration—is usually more satisfying for participants than material reparation. The outcome of the conference belongs to the participants.

Plans for monetary restitution or service should include exact amounts and schedules for completion and specify who will supervise and monitor the agreements. Ideally monitors should be conference participants, not the facilitator or other professionals. A plan for what should happen if the offender fails to complete the agreement might also be included.

Closing the Conference

Before closing, facilitators should ensure that all participants have had a chance to express themselves. After the agreement is finalized and before formally closing the conference, facilitators should give everyone a final opportunity to speak. Facilitators should then thank participants for their contributions, invite them to have refreshments and ask them to stay until they have signed the written conference agreement.

8. CLOSING THE CONFERENCE

"Before I formally close this conference, I would like to provide everyone with a final opportunity to speak. Is there anything anyone wants to say?"

Allow for participants to respond and when they are done, say:

"Thank you for your contributions in dealing with this difficult matter. Congratulations on the way you have worked through the issues. Please help yourselves to some refreshments while I prepare the agreement."

Allow participants ample time to have refreshments and interact. The informal period after the formal conference is very important.

The informal period after the conference, when refreshments are served, is critical to the conference process. It should never be omitted. Much reintegration can occur during this time. Participants generally feel relief that the difficult conference process is over and even satisfaction and enjoyment that they successfully developed and agreed upon a plan to repair the harm.

Refreshments need not be elaborate. For the typical conference, a cold beverage and pretzels or cookies should suffice. In very large conferences, which tend to run longer, the facilitator should probably add something more substantial, such as coffee and pastries.

Facilitators should complete the conference agreement, obtain signatures from the necessary participants and give copies of the agreement to everyone who needs one. Facilitators should say good-bye to all participants as they leave and thank them again for their participation.

Other Points About Facilitating Conferences

Surprises. Occasionally an unexpected revelation occurs. For example, someone may say that they have been sexually abused, or the offender may disclose that they have committed other offenses. When the revelation is particularly serious and overshadows the conference, the facilitator should stop the conference. In other cases, it may be sufficient to acknowledge the revelation and continue.

If the facilitator is a police officer, and a serious offense is revealed in the conference, by either the offender in the conference or by another participant, the officer needs to recognize that person's legal rights. Other facilitators may need to contact the police about the offense. In many jurisdictions where there are laws governing mediation and alternative dispute resolution, disclosures made during a conference will not be admissible in court. Facilitators should know their local laws. However, these laws may not have been adequately tested in the courts.

Varying from the script. While facilitators are advised to stay with the script, within that framework there are occasions when facilitators must improvise. In general, facilitators should speak simply and clearly, avoiding bureaucratic, legalistic or professional jargon. Facilitators should never condescend or patronize and should avoid mimicking the mannerisms and expressions of participants. When facilitators need to paraphrase questions to help someone understand what is being asked, they should ask open-ended questions, which elicit more than a "multiple choice" or "yes or no" answer.

Allowing for emotion. Conference participants should be free to express the full range of emotions. While this may feel uncomfortable at times, it is absolutely necessary for successful conferences. No "ground rules," per se, are established at the beginning of the conference. Ground rules about not raising one's voice or not saying anything negative about someone can deny participants the opportunity to deal with their legitimate anger and constrain how they express themselves.

Only when emotions are expressed in a stigmatizing or abusive way should facilitators intervene. Facilitators should not be too quick to refocus the discussion, however, because other participants may intervene first.

Facilitators should allow substantial time for participants to express their thoughts and feelings and should not avoid or intervene in highly emotional exchanges. Some participants may cry, a natural response to a distressing situation. Crying can greatly impact the offender and others in the conference. When a person is crying, the facilitator should allow silence and can quietly offer that person a tissue.

Redirecting eye contact. Often participants will speak directly to facilitators when answering questions, inhibiting group interaction. To discourage this, facilitators can look at their scripts or other participants. For example, if an offender expresses remorse about the offense, the facilitator can look at the victim to encourage the offender to address that victim.

Inappropriate signs of approval. When questioning participants, facilitators may be tempted to nod their heads in support. Others may see this as approval or agreement and think the facilitator is partial. Therefore, facilitators should avoid nodding their heads when participants speak.

Laughter and humor. Participants may sometimes laugh or joke. As with other emotional expressions, laughter can be appropriate in a conference, often bringing participants a sense of relief.

Profanity. Sometimes conference participants will use profanity, usually in anger. In general, facilitators should not worry about this. However, if the language persists and is abusive or offensive to others, the facilitator may intervene if others do not.

Use of silence. Silence is powerful. Silence emphasizes the impact of comments, allows participants to reflect, enables facilitators to collect their thoughts or determine how to refocus discussion, permits participants to regain their composure and shifts the emphasis toward non-verbal communication.

Translators in conferences. Sometimes a participant may speak little or no English. Facilitators can enlist that participant's relative or friend or a neutral third party to translate. Facilitators should allow extra time between questions for translation.

Arranging further services for participants. Conference participants sometimes bring up problems or issues not directly related to the incident or requiring more substantial attention than the conference can provide. Depending on the setting and the facilitators' experience, facilitators may recommend and refer conference participants to services addressing these issues. Facilitators may even know how to obtain financial support for such services. It is usually best for facilitators to offer referrals outside the formal conference, perhaps during a preconference meeting or after the conference. This ensures that facilitators will not be seen as an ally of a particular person or group.

CHAPTER 5

Establishing a Conferencing Program

Getting Trained

While some will facilitate a conference (or a modified version) after hearing the process described, and others will try conferencing after reading this handbook, most want formal training first.

Real Justice offers a two-day conference facilitator training, which includes videos, role plays and this handbook. Trainees see video of actual conferences, facilitate a role-played conference using the script, participate in several role plays and experience different conference roles—victim, victim supporter, offender and offender supporter. Trainees can also ask questions and get answers from experienced trainers who have facilitated conferences.

Start Facilitating Conferences

To establish a conference program, individuals should start by facilitating a conference, picking one case or incident and simply taking the risk. Recently trained facilitators should run a conference within 30 days of the training, while the experience is fresh in their minds. First-time facilitators commonly report that "it was a textbook conference" because they usually go well. For the unfortunate few who have a less positive experience in their first conferences, the next will likely be "textbook."

If a group from the same organization attends a training, the first to facilitate a conference inspires others to do the same. Group members can sit in on each other's conferences, as observers outside the circle, and provide constructive feedback.

After doing several conferences, facilitators may invite others from their organization, particularly the leadership, to sit in and observe an actual conference. Showing people an actual conference is the best way to overcome their resistance. When an observer attends, facilitators should tell participants who the observer is and ask if they object. Almost invariably, participants will not object.

Defining the Program

The program should now be more clearly defined. Some questions to be answered include:

> Who will refer cases to be conferenced?
> Which cases should be conferenced?
> What criteria will be applied?
> How will cases be referred and tracked?
> What are the parameters?
> Who will facilitate the conferences?
> How will the flow of cases be managed?
> Who will monitor the agreements?

This handbook cannot answer these questions because they depend on the organization, setting, political climate and many other variables. For help with these issues, program organizers can contact the IIRP office.

Handling Participant Refusals

Because conferencing is voluntary, one or more potential participants may refuse to participate. When they are not critical to the conference, it can proceed. When the primary victim or offender decline, some programs ask them to participate instead in a hearing or panel proceeding. When the primary victim declines participation, facilitators may hold a conference with offenders, their supporters and secondary victims.

Ideally, hearings or panel proceedings will incorporate many elements of a restorative process. The hearing officer or panel members can ask the offender, the victim and others questions normally asked in a conference, fostering many of the same dynamics and outcomes.

CHAPTER 6

Restorative Practices: Beyond the Formal Conference

The following chapter is an adaptation of a paper that was presented by Ted Wachtel at the "Reshaping Australian Institutions Conference: Restorative Justice and Civil Society," Australian National University, Canberra, February 16-18, 1999.

Punitive Versus Permissive

Punishment in response to crime and other wrongdoing is the prevailing practice, not just in criminal justice systems but throughout most modern societies. Punishment is usually seen as the most appropriate response to crime and to wrongdoing in schools, families and workplaces. Those who fail to punish naughty children and offending youths and adults are often labelled as "permissive."

PUNITIVE-PERMISSIVE CONTINUUM
Figure 6

PUNITIVE   PERMISSIVE

This punitive-permissive continuum (Figure 6) reflects the current popular view, but offers a very confined perspective and limited choice—to punish or not to punish. The only variable is the severity of the punishment, such as the amount of the fine or the length of the sentence. A more useful view of social discipline can be constructed by looking at the interplay of two more comprehensive variables, control and support.

Social Discipline Window
"Control" is defined as discipline or limit-setting and "support" as encouragement or nurturing. Now a high or low level of control can be combined with a high or low level of support to identify four general approaches to social discipline: neglectful, permissive, punitive (or retributive) and restorative (adapted by P. McCold & T. Wachtel from Glaser, 1969).

The traditional punitive-permissive continuum is subsumed within this more inclusive framework. The permissive approach (lower right of Figure 7) is comprised of low control and high support, a scarcity of limit-setting and an abundance of nurturing. Opposite permissive (upper left of Figure 7) is the punitive (or retributive) approach, high on control and low on support. Sadly, schools and courts in the United States and other countries have increasingly embraced the punitive approach, suspending and expelling more students and imprisoning more citizens than ever before. The third approach, when there is an absence of both limit-setting and nurturing, is neglectful (lower left of Figure 7).

THE SOCIAL DISCIPLINE WINDOW
Figure 7

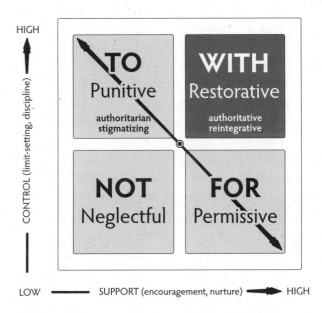

The fourth possibility is restorative (upper right of Figure 7), the approach to social discipline exemplified by Real Justice conferencing. Employing both high control and high support, the restorative approach confronts and disapproves of wrongdoing while supporting and valuing the intrinsic worth of the wrongdoer.

"Control" suggests high control of wrongdoing, not control of human beings in general. The ultimate goal is freedom from the kind of control that wrongdoers impose on others.

This Social Discipline Window can represent parenting styles. For example, there are neglectful parents who are absent, or abusive and permissive parents who are ineffectual or enabling. The term "authoritarian" has been used to describe the punitive parent, while the restorative parent has been called "authoritative" (Baumrind, 1989). Further, one can apply John Braithwaite's (1989) terms to the window: "stigmatizing" responses to wrongdoing are punitive while "reintegrative" responses are restorative.

A few key words—NOT, FOR, TO and WITH—were initially introduced to help clarify the implications of the Social Discipline Window for the staff at the Community Service Foundation's schools and group homes. [Ted Wachtel, one of the authors of this book, founded Community Service Foundation, with his wife, Susan, in 1977.] If the staff were neglectful toward the troubled youth in the agency's programs, they would NOT do anything in response to inappropriate behavior. If permissive, they would do everything FOR the young people in the programs, but ask little in return. If punitive, the staff would respond only by doing things TO the youth. But responding in a restorative manner, they do things WITH the young people when they are inappropriate and involve them directly in the process. A critical element of the restorative approach is that, whenever possible, WITH also includes victims, family, friends and community—those who have been affected by the offender's behavior.

Limitations of Formal Rituals

Although the restorative approach to social discipline expands the options beyond the traditional punitive-permissive continuum, the implementation of restorative justice to date has been narrowly restricted. Restorative justice is usually conceptualized in the form of community service projects designed to reintegrate offenders or formal rituals such as victim-offender mediation, sentencing circles and restorative conferences.

John Braithwaite, in his keynote address at the first North American Conference on Conferencing, asserted that "restorative justice will never become a mainstream alternative to retributive justice unless long-term R[esearch] and D[evelopment] programs show that it does have the capacity to reduce crime" (Braithwaite,

1998). If so, restorative justice as presently practiced is doomed to a peripheral role at the fringes of criminal justice and school disciplinary systems. There is all sorts of evidence that victims, offenders and their respective supporters find restorative justice rituals satisfying and just, but no one has yet conclusively demonstrated that restorative justice rituals significantly reduce reoffense rates or otherwise prevent crime.

Perhaps it is naive to think that a single restorative intervention can change the behavior and mindset of delinquent and high-risk youths, such as those who participate in Community Service Foundation (CSF) counseling, educational and residential programs. Yet young people who attend CSF programs do demonstrate significant positive behavior change. This is because, as Terry O'Connell remarked when he first visited one of the CSF schools in 1995, "You are running a conference all day long." Although the Foundation's staff never used the term "restorative justice" to describe its programs, there is now a growing realization that the Foundation's programs are characterized by the everyday use of a wide range of informal and formal restorative practices.

Restorative Practices Continuum

The term "restorative practice" includes any response to wrongdoing that falls within the parameters defined by the Social Discipline Window as both supportive and limit-setting. After examination, the possibilities become virtually unlimited. To illustrate, one can cite examples from everyday life in CSF's schools and group homes and place those along the restorative practices continuum (see Figure 8).

Moving from the left end of the continuum to the right, the restorative interventions become increasingly formal, involve more people, more planning, more time, are more complete in dealing with the offense, more structured, and due to all of those factors, may have more impact on the offender.

THE RESTORATIVE PRACTICES CONTINUUM
Figure 8

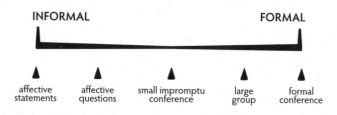

INFORMAL				FORMAL
affective statements	affective questions	small impromptu conference	large group	formal conference

On the far left of the continuum is a simple affective response in which the wronged person lets the offender know how he or she feels about the incident. For example, one of the CSF staff might say, "Jason, you really hurt my feelings when you act like that. And it surprises me, because I don't think you want to hurt anyone on purpose." And that's all that is said. If a similar behavior happens again, the staff person might repeat the response or try a different restorative intervention, perhaps asking, "How do you think Mark felt when you did that?" and then waiting patiently for an answer.

In the middle of the continuum is the small impromptu conference, such as that facilitated by the CSF residential program director, while awaiting a court hearing about placing a 14-year-old boy in a CSF group home. His grandmother told the program director how on Christmas eve, several days before, the boy had gone over to a cousin's house without permission and without letting her know. He did not come back until the next morning, just barely in time for them to catch a bus to her sister's house for Christmas dinner. The program director got the grandmother talking about how that incident had affected her and how worried she was about her grandson. The boy was surprised by how deeply his behavior had affected his grandmother. He readily apologized.

Close to the far right of the continuum is a larger, more formal group process, still short of the formal conference. Two boys got into a fistfight, an unusual event at the CSF schools. After the fight was stopped, their parents were called to come and pick them up. If the boys wanted to return to the school, each boy had to phone and ask for an opportunity to convince the staff and his fellow students that he should be allowed back. Both boys called and came to school. One refused to take responsibility and had a defiant attitude. He was not re-admitted. The other was humble, even tearful. He listened attentively while staff and students told him how he had affected them, willingly took responsibility for his behavior and got a lot of compliments about how he handled the meeting. He was re-admitted and no further action was taken. The other boy was put in the juvenile detention center by his probation officer. Ideally, the probation officer would arrange for a formal restorative conference under the auspices of the court, to address the probation violation, although that is not a normal practice at this time.

One can create informal restorative interventions simply by asking offenders questions from the scripted formal conference. "What happened?" "What were you thinking about at the time?" "Who do you think has been affected?" "How have they been affected?" Whenever possible, one provides those who have been affected with an opportunity to express their feelings to the offenders. The cumulative result of all of this affective exchange in a school is far more productive than lecturing, scolding, threatening or handing out detentions, suspensions and expulsions. The CSF teachers claim that classroom decorum in the CSF schools for troubled youth is better than in the local public schools. But interestingly, CSF staff rarely hold formal conferences. They have found that the more they rely on informal restorative practices in everyday life, the less they need formal restorative rituals.

In the Workplace

Restorative justice is a philosophy, not a model, and ought to guide the way one acts in all of one's dealings. In that spirit, an organization should use restorative practices with staff issues. The leadership should strive for an atmosphere where problems with staff are addressed in a restorative way, where staff can comfortably express concerns and criticisms of the leadership and where leaders are willing to admit and take responsibility for their own mistakes.

Several CSF employees became engaged in a squabble that was disrupting the workplace. The director felt removed enough from the situation to act as facilitator in a conference to deal with the spiraling conflict. In this conference there was no clearly identified wrongdoer. Rather, when invited to the conference, participants were each asked to take as much responsibility as possible for their part in the problem and were assured that everyone else was being asked to do the same. There was a lot of self-disclosure and honesty in the preliminary discussions with each participant. The conference itself exceeded everyone's expectations. Not only did a great deal of healing taking place during the conference, but several individuals made plans to get together one-to-one to further resolve their differences. The conflict became ancient history and was no longer a factor in the CSF workplace.

At Home

Restorative practices are contagious, spreading from workplace to home. A woman related how she, her husband and her younger son restoratively confronted her young adult son, who had just entered the world of work. They told him how annoyed they were with his failure to get himself up on time in the morning. The parents expressed their embarrassment that their son had been late to work at a company where they knew a lot of his coworkers. They insisted that they were stepping back. If their son lost his job, it was not their problem but his. As a result of the informal family group conference, the young man now sets three alarm clocks and gets to work on time.

A police officer who was trained in conferencing shared how he confronted his little boy, who had torn off a piece of new wallpaper, with questions from the conference. The youngster became very remorseful and acknowledged that he had hurt his mother, who loved the new wallpaper, and the workman he had watched put up the new wallpaper. The father felt satisfied that the intervention was far more effective than an old-fashioned scolding or punishment.

Varied Restorative Interventions

A police officer ran a variation on a restorative conference with a dispute between neighbors about a barking dog; another held an impromptu conference on the front porch between a homeowner and an adolescent prankster who stole a lawn ornament. Still another police officer held a conference for the families of two run-aways, helping the teen-agers' understanding of how hurtful their actions were, although they had not committed a criminal offense that would typically require the officer's involvement. An assistant principal made two teen-agers, on the verge of a fight, tell each other how they were feeling and brought them to quick resolution. A corrections officer addressed an inmate's angry outburst with a conference. A social worker got family members talking to each other in a real way about a teen-ager's persistent truancy and got the youth to start going to school. Beyond the formal criminal justice ritual, there are an infinite number of opportunities for restorative interventions.

Basics of Restorative Practice

For restorative practices to be effective in changing offender behavior, one should try to do the following:

1. **Foster awareness.** In the most basic intervention simply ask a few questions of the offender that foster awareness of how others have been affected by the wrongdoing. Or express one's own feelings to the offender. In more elaborate

interventions one can provide an opportunity for others to express their feelings to the offenders.

2. **Avoid scolding or lecturing.** When offenders are exposed to other people's feelings and discover how victims and others have been affected by their behavior, they feel empathy for others. When scolded or lectured, they react defensively. They see themselves as victims and are distracted from noticing other people's feelings.

3. **Involve offenders actively.** All too often authorities try to hold offenders accountable by simply doling out punishment. But in a punitive intervention, offenders are completely passive. They just sit quietly and act like victims. In a restorative intervention, offenders are usually asked to speak. They face and listen to victims and others whom they have affected. They help decide how to repair the harm and must then keep their commitments. Offenders have an active role in a restorative process and are truly held accountable.

4. **Accept ambiguity.** Sometimes, as in a fight between two people, fault is unclear. In those cases one may have to accept ambiguity. Privately, before the conference, encourage individuals to take as much responsibility as possible for their part in the conflict. Even when offenders do not fully accept responsibility, victims often want to proceed. As long as everyone is fully informed of the ambiguous situation in advance, the decision to proceed with a restorative intervention belongs to the participants.

5. **Separate the deed from the doer.** In an informal intervention, either privately with the offenders or publicly after the victims are feeling some resolution, express the

assumption that the offenders did not mean to harm anyone or express surprise that the offenders would do something like that. When appropriate, one may want to cite some of their virtues or accomplishments. The goal is to recognize the offenders' worth and disapprove only of their wrongdoing.

6. **See every instance of wrongdoing and conflict as an opportunity for learning.** The teacher in the classroom, the police officer in the community, the probation officer with his caseload and the corrections officer in the prison all have opportunities to model and teach. They can turn negative incidents into constructive events—building empathy and a sense of community, which reduces the likelihood of negative incidents in the future.

The value of restorative practices in addressing crime and wrongdoing is not based on theory or wishful thinking but on the results at CSF schools, group homes and other programs. Juvenile courts and schools from throughout eastern Pennsylvania send CSF 500 of their more troublesome young people at any one time. Thanks to restorative practices, these youth change their behaviors, cooperate, take positive leadership roles and confront each other about inappropriate behavior.

The CSF staff lacked an adequate way of expressing why these changes occurred until encountering the concept of restorative justice. CSF and its sister organization, Buxmont Academy, has undertaken a research project to evaluate more specifically how the agencies' use of restorative practices impacts young people, what specifically changes and to what extent those changes are sustained after students and clients leave CSF.

The evaluation has been undertaken in three parts (McCold, 2002, 2004; McCold & Chang, 2008). Overall, it has tracked 3,928 youth discharged from CSF Buxmont programs from 1999 through 2006, showing a remarkable decrease in offending among these youth. The first study, conducted 1999–2001, employed evaluation protocols developed by Temple University's Crime and Justice Research Center and tracked 919 youth. Besides significant lowered offending rates, the study showed enhanced pro-social attitudes and improved self-esteem among students immersed in the restorative environments of CSF Buxmont programs. The second study, conducted 2001–2003, replicated the same findings vis-à-vis offending with a new sample of 858 youth and also followed up with the original population of 919, finding that the effect of restorative practices persisted two years after program discharge. The third study, 2003–2006, tracked 2,151 youth 2, 6 and 12 months after program discharge and found that offending decreased at the same significant rate, demonstrating a lasting program effect.

The Community Service Foundation was the sponsoring agency for the Real Justice program and has subsidized its efforts since 1995. As Real Justice progressed in its efforts, training thousands in conference facilitation skills, it became apparent that many trainees never conducted a conference. Some hesitated to facilitate a formal conference because they were afraid. Others did not have the authority to bypass existing procedures and sanctions, such as zero tolerance policies in schools. Nonetheless a large number of people have implemented restorative practices, using elements of the conference process informally as discussed above.

So Real Justice added the concept of restorative practices to its trainings, specifically encouraging people to try less formal interventions when they cannot do conferences. The idea has been well received, particularly among educators. While many teachers and administrators claimed that they did not have time or the right circumstance to pull together a full-blown conference, they were enthusiastic about more spontaneous restorative strategies. As a result of this positive response, Real Justice developed the

SaferSanerSchools™ program to help educators implement a range of restorative practices in schools.

Police officers, probation officers, correctional officers and others have also faced obstacles in implementing conferencing. They may choose to proceed by using informal practices as a way to start making their own institutions and systems more restorative.

In 1999 Ted Wachtel founded the International Institute for Restorative Practices (IIRP), a nonprofit educational organization, to take over the ongoing Real Justice® and SaferSanerSchools™ programs, as well as two additional programs, Family Power℠, to address restorative practices in social work and counseling, and Good Company℠, focusing on organizational management. The IIRP collaborates with the Community Service Foundation and Buxmont Academy, which serve as demonstration programs for the use of restorative practices. In 2006 the Pennsylvania Department of Education authorized the IIRP as a specialized research and graduate degree–granting institution, the first graduate school in the world wholly dedicated to restorative practices.

References

Baumrind, D. (1989, August 19). Presentation of an ongoing study at the 1989 American Psychological Association annual meeting, New Orleans, LA, as reported by B. Bower, Teenagers reap broad benefits from 'authoritative' parents. *Science News*, Vol. 136.

Braithwaite, J. (1989). *Crime, shame and reintegration*. New York: Cambridge University Press.

Braithwaite, J. (1998, August 6-8). Linking crime prevention to restorative justice. Presented at the First North American Conference on Conferencing, Minneapolis, MN.

Glaser, D. (1969). *The effectiveness of a prison and parole system*, pp. 289-297. Indianapolis, IN: Bobbs-Merrill.

McCold, P. (2004, November). Evaluation of a restorative milieu: Replication and extension for 2001-2003 discharges. Paper presented at the annual meeting of the American Society of Criminology, Nashville, TN. [http://www.realjustice.org/library/erm2.html]

McCold, P. (2002, November). Evaluation of a restorative milieu: CSF Buxmont school/day treatment programs, 1999-2001. Paper presented at the American Society of Criminology Annual Meeting, Chicago, IL. [http://www.realjustice.org/library/erm.html]

McCold, P. & Wachtel, B. (1998). *Restorative policing experiment: The Bethlehem, Pennsylvania, police family group conferencing project.* A report to the National Institute of Justice, U.S. Department of Justice, Washington, DC.

McCold, P. & Chang, A. (2008, June 9). Community Service Foundation and Buxmont Academy analysis of students discharged during three school years (2003–2006). *Restorative Practices eForum.* [http://www.realjustice.org/library/csf_2007.html]

Moore, D.B. & Forsythe, L. (1995). *A new approach to juvenile justice: An evaluation of family conferencing in Wagga Wagga.* A report to the Criminology Research Council. Wagga Wagga, New South Wales, Australia: Centre for Rural Social Research, Charles Sturt University-Riverina.

Nathanson, D. (1992). *Shame and pride: Affect, sex and the birth of the self.* New York: Norton & Company.

Umbreit, M. & Fercello, C. (1998). Family group conferencing program results in client satisfaction. *Juvenile Justice Update,* December/January 1998, pp. 3–4, 12–13.

Umbreit, M. & Fercello, C. (1999). *Client evaluation of family group conferencing in 12 sites in 1st judicial district of Minnesota.* Center for Restorative Justice and Mediation, School of Social Work, University of Minnesota.

Zehr, H. (1990). *Changing lenses: A new focus for crime and justice.* Scottdale, PA: Herald Press.

Educational Resources

To learn more about DVDs, books and
other resources provided by the IIRP,
please go to **www.iirp.org/store**.

DVDs

Burning Bridges

"Burning Bridges" is a 35-minute documentary about the arson of Mood's Bridge, a historic covered bridge in Bucks County, Pennsylvania, USA, and the restorative conference held in its wake. The International Institute for Restorative Practices facilitated this emotional conference, which brought together the six young men who burned down the bridge with their families and members of the community. Using news footage, interviews and video of the actual conference, the documentary tells the story of a community moving through grief and anger to healing.

Four School Conferences: A Composite View

Four actual Real Justice conferences were videotaped, with the permission of participants, at alternative schools operated by the Community Service Foundation and Buxmont Academy, sister nonprofit organizations serving troubled youth in eastern Pennsylvania. Footage from the conferences, which were held for offenses ranging from truancy and leaving school grounds to drug possession and bringing a knife onto a school bus, provide viewers with a realistic view of conferencing. Some conferences are highly emotional; others are not. Some conferences produce satisfying outcomes; others are less successful. But follow-up interviews with conference participants show that even a so-called "unsuccessful" conference can produce meaningful outcomes.

Toxic Talk

"Toxic Talk" shows an actual restorative conference following a workplace incident, in which staff members demeaned their supervisor behind her back and in the presence of customers. The conference, by providing everyone involved with a structured setting to express their emotions freely and honestly, transformed the negative feelings created by the incident into positive ones. The process restored relationships and created a healthier work environment.

DVDs

Facing the Demons

"Facing the Demons" documents the journey of the family and friends of murdered victim Michael Marslew, confronting face-to-face in a conference two of the offenders responsible for Michael's death.

Produced by the Dee Cameron Company, "Facing the Demons" won an award for "best television documentary of 1999" at the 2000 Logies Awards, the Australian equivalent of the Emmy Award, and in 2000 earned the United Nations Association Award for Best Television in its annual Media Peace Awards.

The 30'-minute companion DVD "Commentary on Facing the Demons: The Facilitator's Perspective" — which includes commentary by Terry O'Connell, the Australian police sergeant who facilitated the dramatic conference — answers questions and addresses issues raised by the documentary.

A free 8-page study guide is available at:
www.iirp.org/pdf/FacingTheDemonsStudyGuide.pdf

Conferencing for Serious Offenses: An Exploration

This thought-provoking, interactive, "do-it-yourself" seminar package provides DVDs (and a CD-ROM with printable Facilitator Guide and Participant Handout) for a group of professionals, students or others to examine the use of restorative conferencing in response to serious offenses.

The seminar package provides detailed directions for using the videos. Also included are instructions on how to run a "circle," which is the format used to structure discussion in the seminar. The use of the circle process provides a truly restorative experience that encourages active participation from everyone attending the seminar.

Please note: *This seminar is not intended to train participants to facilitate restorative conferences, but to enhance their understanding of the potential and the implications of conferencing for serious offenses.*

Books

The Restorative Practices Handbook for Teachers, Disciplinarians and Administrators

"The Restorative Practices Handbook" is a practical guide for educators interested in implementing restorative practices, an approach that proactively builds positive school communities while dramatically reducing discipline referrals, suspensions and expulsions. The handbook discusses the spectrum of restorative techniques, offers implementation guidelines, explains how and why the processes work, and relates real-world stories of restorative practices in action.

Safer Saner Schools: Restorative Practices in Education

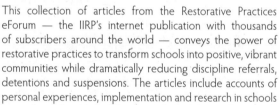

This collection of articles from the Restorative Practices eForum — the IIRP's internet publication with thousands of subscribers around the world — conveys the power of restorative practices to transform schools into positive, vibrant communities while dramatically reducing discipline referrals, detentions and suspensions. The articles include accounts of personal experiences, implementation and research in schools from the United States and Canada to the United Kingdom, Europe, Australia and Asia.

Other Resources

Restorative Questions Poster

This 18" x 24" poster, designed for use in classrooms, prominently displays the essential restorative questions for easy reference in the event of a conflict or harmful incident. The top has questions used to respond to challenging behavior; the bottom has questions to help those harmed by others' actions.

Restorative Questions Sign

This rugged, portable 20" x 35" A-frame sign is designed for use in schools and on playgrounds. It prominently displays the essential restorative questions for easy reference in the event of a conflict or harmful incident. One side has questions used to respond to challenging behavior; the other has questions to help those harmed by others' actions.

Restorative Questions Cards

This pack of 100 handy two-sided coated 2" x 3.5" cards puts the essential restorative questions at your fingertips. One side has questions used to respond to challenging behavior; the other has questions to help those harmed by others' actions. The cards fit easily in a wallet.

IIRP Globe Ball

This small, squeezable globe ball is perfect for use as a talking piece in restorative circles.

Visit **www.iirp.org/store**

Join the IIRP's Restorative Practices eForum

Be part of a worldwide network of people who are interested in restorative practices. Receive hopeful, useful news about restorative practices efforts in education, criminal justice, family and social services and the workplace.

The Restorative Practices eForum is a free email information service provided by the IIRP. The eForum provides members with occasional short emails that include brief summaries of significant articles, research reports or information about upcoming restorative practices events — with links to full articles.

eForum emails do not include attachments. We do not share our eForum database, so you will receive no spam.

Sign up and view past articles — many of which contain more detailed information about processes described in this book — at **www.iirp.org/eforum**.

About the IIRP

This volume is presented by the International Institute for Restorative Practices (IIRP), the world's first graduate school wholly dedicated to the emerging field of restorative practices. The IIRP is engaged in the advanced education of professionals at the graduate level and to the conduct of research that can develop the growing field of restorative practices, with the goal of positively influencing human behavior and strengthening civil society throughout the world. The IIRP offers master's degree and certificate programs for educators and others who work with children and youth. To learn more about the IIRP Graduate School, go to **www.iirp.org**.

The IIRP Training and Consulting Division is the leading world provider of restorative practices training, consulting and international conferences, as well as print, video and other resources. The IIRP and its related organizations have trained thousands of individuals in education, criminal justice, and social and human services since its inception as the Real Justice program in 1995. To learn more about the IIRP Training and Consulting Division, go to **www.iirp.org/training**.

About the Authors

Ted Wachtel is the president and founder of the IIRP. In 1977, Wachtel and his wife, Susan, founded the Community Service Foundation and Buxmont Academy, which operate schools, foster group homes and other programs in Pennsylvania — which employ restorative practices with delinquent and at-risk youth. Wachtel's publications include *Toughlove*, the best-selling book for parents of troubled adolescents, *Real Justice* and the *Conferencing Handbook*, as well as numerous book chapters and journal articles. He has been a guest speaker at conferences on restorative practices around the world.

Terry O'Connell pioneered restorative justice in Australia, the United Kingdom and North America. He is responsible for the Real Justice model of restorative conferencing. A 30-year police veteran, he worked with Thames Valley Police service developing restorative practices in the U.K., including its use in police complaints/discipline systems. Terry now works across a range of family, community, institutional and workplace settings. He received the Order of Australia medal and was recently awarded an Honorary Doctorate from Catholic University in Sydney, Australia.

Ben Wachtel is director of communications and technology for the IIRP. He has worked with the IIRP since its inception and its sister organizations, Community Service Foundation and Buxmont Academy, since 1995. Ben served as a researcher on the Restorative Policing Experiment, a National Institute of Justice–funded study of the Bethlehem Police Department's restorative justice conferencing program with juvenile offenders, completed in 1998.